Christian Symbol and Ritual

Christian Symbol and Ritual

An Introduction

BERNARD COOKE

GARY MACY

OXFORD

UNIVERSITY PRESS

2005

OXFORD
UNIVERSITY PRESS

Oxford University Press, Inc., publishes works that further
Oxford University's objective of excellence
in research, scholarship, and education.

Oxford   New York
Auckland   Cape Town   Dar es Salaam   Hong Kong   Karachi
Kuala Lumpur   Madrid   Melbourne   Mexico City   Nairobi
New Delhi   Shanghai   Taipei   Toronto

With offices in
Argentina   Austria   Brazil   Chile   Czech Republic   France   Greece
Guatemala   Hungary   Italy   Japan   Poland   Portugal   Singapore
South Korea   Switzerland   Thailand   Turkey   Ukraine   Vietnam

Copyright © 2005 by Oxford University Press, Inc.

Published by Oxford University Press, Inc.
198 Madison Avenue, New York, New York 10016

www.oup.com

Oxford is a registered trademark of Oxford University Press

Library of Congress Cataloging-in-Publication Data
Cooke, Bernard J.
Christian symbol and ritual: an introduction / Bernard Cooke and Gary Macy.
   p. cm.
Includes bibliographical references and index.
ISBN-13 978-0-19-515411-5; 978-0-19-515412-2 (pbk.)
ISBN 0-19-515411-8; 0-19-515412-6 (pbk.)
1. Liturgics.   2. Ritual.   3. Christian art and symbolism.   4. Theology, doctrinal.
I. Macy, Gary.   II. Title.
BV178.C66 2005
264—dc22   2004029400

9 8 7 6 5 4 3 2 1

Printed in the United States of America
on acid-free paper

To Pauline Turner and Saralynn Ferrara

Preface

This is a book born directly from the classroom. We were both teaching courses on the sacraments at the University of San Diego a few years back (in one case together), and both came to similar conclusions.

First, the student body had changed dramatically over the last few decades. More and more students were coming from families that had little or no regular religious practice. While the students might consider themselves to be generically Christian or even specifically Lutheran Christians, Roman Catholic Christians, and so on, they had little or no understanding of their own traditions. One such student, when she was assigned to read the Gospels, was shocked to find out Jesus died. A teacher simply could not take any Christian background for granted. Many students were unchurched in any sense. They and their families practiced and professed no religion at all. The books we used to teach our courses, while excellent in themselves, simply assumed too much on the part of the students. They used words like "sacrament" or "grace" or "salvation" as if the student already knew what these words meant. Quite likely at the time when the texts were written, this was a fair assumption. Times, however, had changed, and so had the students.

Second, most of the books on Christian rituals were books written from a Roman Catholic perspective deliberately for Roman Catholics. There were few, if any, books written to introduce Christian rituals in general, at least not books for undergraduate students.

We decided to do our best, therefore, to write a book that had two aims: first, to write an introduction to Christian ritual that assumed the reader had little or no background in Christianity; second, to write a book that attempted to introduce the reader to Christian ritual in general. During the process of writing, different sections were used in class and tested and refined, as it were, under fire. Insofar as this small sample of students is useful, the method seemed to work.

When a writer attempts to take nothing for granted, and when a text is tempered by the questions of the classroom, the text tends to be written with a kind of anticipation. Most chapters include not only a description of a particular Christian ritual but also a theology to explain that ritual, as well as the historical background to explicate the debates that still roil Christians concerning those rituals. We are attempting to answer the readers' inevitable "but" questions: "But then why do some Christians baptize children, while others don't?" "But why then is Sunday service different at my church?" "But why do some Christians have priests and some ministers?" This means the chapters may well seem to drift away from a discussion of ritual per se. We can also beg for your patience. We may be answering someone else's "but" question rather than yours at the moment.

Another ultimate and practical purpose also motivated composition of the book. In recent decades there has been a noticeable movement toward people's increased activity in worship services. Pentecostal services have proved attractive to thousands. In Roman Catholicism, the Second Vatican Council made a historic and revolutionary shift in its explanation of desirable Eucharistic celebration, a shift from people "attending" Mass that is celebrated by an ordained liturgical "specialist" to people's active participation in the celebration: a shift from spectacle to ritual. However—and the council's document on the liturgy states this emphatically—people can share consciously, intelligently, and effectively in ritual only if they know what ritual is and what their function in the Eucharistic ritual is. We hope this book can help create such an understanding of ritual.

While clearly written by Roman Catholics, and while using Roman Catholicism as the main examples, we hope that this will be a book that would be accessible to all Christians. With over 130 years of Catholic life and experience between us, our biases cannot help but show. We trust that these inevitable predispositions will not alienate or offend.

A book such as this owes so much to so many that it would hard to mention all the influences that have shaped our thought over many years. We should at least like to mention, however, Orlando Espín, Michael Lawler, Susan Ross, Kenan Osborne, Geoffrey Wainwright, Catherine Bell, Bruce Morrill, Joseph Powers, Raul Gómez, Dennis Krause, and Phyllis Zagano. Finally, we thank Cynthia Read from Oxford University Press who encouraged us throughout the process and waited patiently for the final product.

Contents

Introduction:
Symbolism, Root of Ritual, 3

1. Characteristics and Functions of Rituals, 19

2. Rituals in the Christian Context, 35

3. Rituals of Friendship, 55

4. Rituals of Christian Initiation, 69

5. Rituals of Prayer, Worship, and the Eucharist, 87

6. Rituals of Reconciliation, 109

7. Rituals of Service and Ministry, 119

8. Rituals for Healing, Suffering, Death, 147

Conclusion:
Christian Life as Ritual, 161

Suggestions for Further Reading, 171

Index, 175

Christian Symbol and Ritual

Introduction

Symbolism, Root of Ritual

When you first opened this book, how did you do it? Just open it up to this page and start reading? Did you carefully open it in the middle first so as not to break the binding? Did you check the notes and bibliography first to get a better idea of what sources the authors used? Did you lick your finger in anticipation of page turning? Did you quickly flip through the chapter headings to get an overall idea of the book?

Maybe you did all or some of the above actions without really thinking about them. It's just a habit after years of reading. You may even have a favorite place and time for reading; the evenings, perhaps, are reserved for novels while you snuggle deep into a favorite chair. Or maybe you have to read this book for a course; then you might be chained to the desk, sitting straight up with pen poised for notes and dread in your heart, faced with another dreary textbook.

Chances are that you have some ritual habits with which you approach a new book. Whether you are aware of it or not, even little actions like picking up a new book usually involve rituals. We hope that this book will make you more aware of how much of life is made up of rituals, and how much those rituals do not just enrich your life but even shape your identity.

Pervasiveness of Symbols

For now, however, it might be valuable just to take a moment and think of the many areas where rituals and symbols help structure one's day and ease one through everyday life. Many people, especially in Western cultures, think of themselves as eminently practical. The actions that make up the bulk of their lives are pragmatic, practical, functional. They are not wrong to think so, but certainly they make a mistake if they think that ritual actions are not pragmatic, practical, and functional. Take these letters as they march across the page: P–A–G–E. Every single one is a symbol. Every word is a symbol; every sentence structures those symbols and is, in this sense, a ritual. Language itself, so basic to human communication and knowledge, is both symbol and ritual. Clearly, language is both symbolic and ritualistic, but at the same time it is eminently practical and functional.

Rituals aid human interaction in other less obvious, but equally important, ways. Quite likely, as you move through your day, you encounter many people that you know and you address them with "Hi, how are you?" or "How's it going?" or "What's up?" or some equivalent. The person so addressed is likely to respond something like, "Great! And how are you?" or perhaps, "Hanging in there" or even "So, so." Now, you probably don't really want to sit down and hear all about that person's present life, although this is actually what you are asking. Nor is it likely that the person really wants to tell you how their life is proceeding, although the responses "Hanging in there" and "So, so" leave open the possibility for further inquiry. What is really taking place here is a ritual. You are letting the person know that you recognize them and that, most likely, you don't have time to talk right now. They are saying that they appreciate the recognition, recognize you back, but, again most likely, don't have time to talk, although again, some responses leave open that possibility.

In fact, it would be annoying if the person responded, "Well, you know, in general, things are good, but lately my lower back has been bothering me a bit and my car has been sounding funny," and then began to describe in detail the problems of their lives. This little ritual is, in fact, a very effective way of being both polite and not getting bogged down in extensive discussions of the lives of all the acquaintances we meet during the day. Of course, you have to be in on the ritual. A friend from Italy used to be infuriated by Americans who asked how she was and then refused to listen to her serious response. She thought we were simply rude and uncaring until this simple ritual of recognition was explained to her. "Well, then, say what you mean," was her response. Of course, we are saying what we mean, not, in this case, what the literal words mean, but what the entire ritual conveys to those who know it.

When you think about ritual in this way, you may begin to notice all the rituals that help ease human contact and communication in extremely helpful ways. In fact, it would be a very useful exercise to start to note the rituals that help you through your particular daily routine. Do you have a ritual you follow when you wake up in the morning? Do you pick out clothes that will tell others who you are? Do you dress as a student or a businessperson or a homemaker? Do you use makeup, wear a tie, or just slap on a pair of jeans? Do you take a ritual break in the middle of the day for lunch or just throw food down at your desk? If you take a few minutes every day and write down all the ritual actions and all the symbols that shape your day, you may find yourself amazed at how important symbols and rituals are to the fundamentally practical and pragmatic people we claim to be.

Of course, there are also the moments in our lives when we are deliberately and self-consciously ritualistic. For most people, the most important rituals in their lives revolve around family, religion, and, oddly, sports. The last suggestion might strike some readers as strange, but sports are pure ritual. Sports celebrate certain values in our society, values we prize highly. However, unlike the rituals mentioned above, they perform no practical function. If one wants, for instance, to move a pigskin spheroid 100 yards, there are plenty of easier and less-expensive ways to do so than by placing several large and very well paid gentlemen in the way. Tennis, as the comedians Flanders and Swan once so inelegantly put it, is fundamentally "smashing the skin of a mouse with the gut of cat." We use much more expensive materials than mouse skin or cat gut these days, but the smashing is the same and when you are done, what do you have? No product has been produced, no person helped, no problem solved, no cure found.

By now, sports fans reading this book are seething and ready to write scathing letters to the authors. Please don't. We understand that sports are very, very important to many people precisely because they are rituals—rituals that many people prize very highly. The proof of this is the large salaries professional athletes earn, as well as the sometime frightening intensity of those who love these rituals (remember that "fan" is simply short for "fanatic"). Sports celebrate competition, intensity, dedication, and individuality, as well as teamwork. Sports also celebrate local identity. A team doesn't lose (in the eyes of a true fan), a city does; a school does; even the individual fan does. Sports are a dramatic example of rituals that are extremely important to people, even though, from an outsider's point of view, they serve no practical function. To the insider, however, they perform a very important function: they celebrate a person's identity and his or her most important values. Sociologists might insist that at least some sports also divert aggression into an acceptable form, provide a diversion from stress, and perform other important societal functions. Indeed, sports do fulfill these roles, and perhaps that is the point to be made. Even "pure ritual" performs important functions.

By now, we hope, the reader has decided that perhaps rituals are not just stuffy, meaningless ceremonies from the past and symbols aren't just arbitrary and useless meanings ascribed to certain objects. Of course, some rituals and symbols are empty and meaningless, although scholars might argue these would not be true rituals or symbols. Unfortunately, for many people, the terms "symbol" and "rituals" always imply those ceremonies and objects that are clearly artificial and imposed. While there are good historical reasons for people to think this way, quite probably people only recognize rituals and symbols as such when they are obviously contrived or have lost their meaningfulness. When rituals and symbols are working and working well in a person's life, they pass by unnoticed as symbols or rituals. In fact, the most powerful symbols and rituals are so central to one's life that one forgets the fact that they are human constructions.

How Do Symbols Work?

Scholars analyze everything, and recently one of the subjects that has most fascinated them is this business of symbols and rituals. Why do humans have symbols? Why do they come up with rituals? How do rituals shape people's lives and even the very way they see the world? Before we can begin to understand how Christians use symbols, it is important to understand a little better what symbols and rituals are in a more general sense, since Christian rituals and symbols are precisely that: part of the whole universe of symbols and rituals used, it seems, by all humans at all times.

The Origin of Symbolism

Susanne Langer,[1] in her book, *Philosophy in a New Key*, made the intriguing proposal that the human person is essentially a symbol-making being. In ar-

---

1. Susanne Langer (1895–1985) was an American philosopher who studied those aspects of human feeling that language doesn't seem to adequately express. She wrote *Philosophy in a New Key: A Study in the Symbolism of Reason, Rite, and Art* (Cambridge, MA.: Harvard University Press, 1957) in 1942.

guing for her position, Langer was basing her thought on a long philosophical tradition reaching back as least as far as the philosopher Immanuel Kant (1724–1804), who did much of his philosophical work around the time of the American Revolution. Kant stressed the fact that human perceptions and understandings of reality shape human reality. In this case, Langer is suggesting that symbols actually shape our reality.

There certainly is a good deal of truth in that claim, and it has been made in slightly different forms by those who see human language as the very heart of human existence. However, it seems that one can go even further and say that the root of all symbolism in human experience and expression is the fact that we humans, because we have physical bodies, necessarily exist symbolically.

Humans Exist Symbolically

Humans are conscious beings, aware and self-aware of their surroundings and even aware of themselves as aware. We have this amazing capacity to somehow bring into ourselves in awareness what exists distinctly outside ourselves. I know that I am not the tree I see, and yet in knowledge I somehow bring that tree into existing as a knower. To put it another way, the only trees I know are trees that are part of and are shaped by my experience. Trees, although not me, exist only as part of my world. Because we are self-aware beings, we experience two kinds of existing: things exist physically, materially, in the world, as indeed do we; at the same time, we exist intentionally in our awareness. In knowledge we endow the things we know with intentional existence—that is, an existence shaped by our experience of and knowledge about those things. We judge that the tree has an existence of its own, but we only know trees as they have influenced our lives, not trees in the abstract.

At the same time, we exist bodily, not just mentally. Even if, as many people have believed and still do believe, humans are basically spirits, the spiritual activity of knowing is knowing carried on while being in a body, at least in this life. There is nothing we know that we do not know through our bodily powers of perception. Even when things have become known to us, translated into our thoughts about them, we cannot think about them without sensible imagery in our imaginations and memory. To use the traditional language of Greek philosophy, we are not body and soul; we are embodied spirits.

By "embodied spirits" is meant simply that as we presently exist we exist in a body and, in fact, barring some claims to very exceptional experiences, without our bodies we would be dead, even for those who believe in life after death. Still, we have the experience as well that our bodies don't exhaust our existence. We are more than our bodies. There is some "self," some "me," that is more than the physical part of us that gets tired, out of shape, or even mangled by an accident. By "spirit" is meant that part of us that is more than just the physical. If you like, it is what separates a corpse from a living person. Some people deny that this part of us is any more than a special function of the body; others claim that this part of us transcends the body and even death and constitutes the real "us."

For the purposes of this book, this debate, however interesting and important, is really irrelevant. Whatever constitutes the spirit of a person, it remains true that the people who perform rituals and use symbols are those who are definitely in their bodies. Rituals and symbols without bodies just don't make sense. This was so clear to medieval writers that they argued that only embodied humans need symbols and rituals. Angels, demons, and even animals don't have them and don't need them. Angels and demons perceive things directly; they don't need the intermediaries of the senses. Animals (at least according to the medieval writers) don't have the kind of minds that would understand symbols or rituals. For animals, it would only be sense data without meaning. So symbols and rituals are distinctive human actions that humans need as long as they need their bodies, and it is humans solidly in their bodies that this book is about.

This is not to deny the importance of that part of ourselves that goes beyond the mere physicality of our bodies. Our very bodiliness is what it is because it is the bodiliness of a spirit. That is why a bodily ailment is felt as pain. That bodiliness translates who we are, so that others can recognize us. Our inner thoughts and emotions are immediately expressed in bodily word and gesture: a raised eyebrow, a smile, and spoken words let others (and often we ourselves) know what is going on "inside" of us. We are living symbols because the perception of our bodily gestures and actions "speaks," or symbolizes, the inner spiritual states that are not directly perceptible to others.

Symbolism of Experience

Our lives as humans are a sequence of experiences, experiences that involve our bodiliness. We are sick or healthy, we are endangered by floods and earthquakes, or we are warmed and relaxed by the sun on a summer day. But because we are also spirits, such happenings are not just happenings, they are experiences. They have meaning for us. And what they mean is intrinsic to the reality of the happening *for us.* What they mean depends on the extent and manner in which we have been conditioned to find a certain meaning in the happening. If I have been brought up to see a tornado as a threat, the appearance of a funnel cloud will carry with it the meaning that danger is imminent, and I will experience being in danger. Because a funnel cloud has had associated with it the destructiveness of a tornado, it symbolizes the danger I fear— and should the tornado actually hit where I am standing, the symbolism becomes greatly enhanced. Even when I am in no danger from a tornado, as in seeing one depicted in a movie, that sight can still cause in me some of the panic of the original happening.

Even our objective and scientific view of the world is one that we have picked up through a particular set of experiences. In science classes in school, or through actual research if one is a scientist, one practices seeing and experiencing the world in a particular way. This approach has had both powerful benefits and distinct disadvantages for humans, but it is not an exception to the general rule that the world we know is one that is shaped by our individual and collective experiences of that world. In short, the scientific world is no closer to the world as it is in itself (whatever that might be) than is the poetic vision of the world. The scientific view merely has a different usefulness for humans than the poetic view. The reason we ascribe more reality to science than to poetry is because our society values science and the benefits science offers more highly than poetry or the benefits poetry offers.

So, depending on the effect they have had, or could have, on our bodiliness—whether pain or pleasure, joy or sorrow, nurture or damage—things or persons or events come to have particular meanings. On the one hand, there are many things that are relatively insignificant and many persons who are not particularly significant in our lives, and so their symbolic power over us is rather minimal. They don't really affect us that much, if at all. On the other hand, there are some persons or happenings that so symbolize happiness or acceptance or achievement that they are a major factor in our establishing a self-identity and reaching maturity. Clearly, some of the effects we have just described have more to do with our spirit than with our bodiliness; happiness that comes with a deep friendship, for example, affects the spirit. But even in this case, awareness of the other's friendship came because bodily symbols like touch or gifts or words were used to convey that other's inner attitude toward one. In sum, things or persons or events begin to take on meaning for a person as he or she experiences them, and so they become symbols of that meaning.

For example, let's say you want to tell your dearest friend that she is much more than "just a friend." In fact, you love her like no one else. You decide to surprise your friend with a beautiful bouquet of long-stemmed red roses. When you get to the florist, you find out to your horror that this will cost you most of your money. Your love is strong, however, and you order the roses and have them sent to your beloved. Alas, you have the misfortune of loving a thoroughgoing practical scientist. When you next meet, you ask if she got the roses. "Yes," the beloved exclaims, "what exquisite specimens. Pity they won't ever go to seed. I mulched them," and absent-mindedly hands you back the card that came with them.

Rage, tears, sadness; all would hardly be out of place, but surely that little card would become a symbol of frustration and long-stemmed red roses would never be the same for you again. Your odd friend, however, would be quite correct in a world where roses are only the reproductive organs of plants. Roses, however, in a truly human world are not just that; they are also a sign of beauty, of love, even in this case of commitment and sacrifice. A rose is rarely just a rose, not for human beings, and roses as known by human beings are the only roses there are. In this case, you might say the poetic vision of roses was, for you if not for your friend, more real than the "objective" scientific view.

Symbols and Shared Experience

One of the amazing features of being human is that we are not limited to our own individual experiences. We can share our experiences, so that to some extent I can experience vicariously what has happened to another. Because of this, what has become meaningful to another can become meaningful to me. And the symbols of that meaning can be shared commonly. Such common appreciation of the meaning conveyed by shared symbols is the basis for the advertising industry, supports the efforts of governments to foster nationalism, and feeds into the metaphors that are central to all true art. Millions of people watching the Superbowl on television see the same TV commercials. Though they do this as individuals, all are sharing the same images—images that symbolize the desirability of the advertised product. That desirability can appeal to most of them because a shared symbol is being used. For example, the scene portrayed in the ad is that of a group of young people on a beach suddenly becoming excited and rushing over to examine the newest model auto that drives up. In a culture where "youth" has become a symbol of carefree life, the message is clear: if you wish to enjoy carefree life, buy the advertised auto. In the example of the rose, the odd person is your beloved scientist. For some reason (and sadly for you), she has not picked up the shared symbolism of our society about roses. If she had, she would have known immediately of your love and sacrifice.

Some of these shared symbols stand out as unifying the understandings and emotions of an entire nation. Because of television, the war in Vietnam was the first war experienced vicariously by people throughout the United States. While this exposure to the reality of modern warfare played a major part in making the war unpopular, one scene in particular symbolized in striking fashion the horror and injustice of civilian suffering in Vietnam. That was the scene of a young girl, fleeing naked down a street, her body seared by napalm. Another instance in which the entire nation shared emotions was the televised funeral of assassinated President John F. Kennedy, the common feelings of bereavement symbolized by the riderless horse in the funeral procession. Most recently, the terrible image of the collapsing twin towers of the World Trade Center in New York haunts the collective memory of the United States.

Symbols tend to be limited to the cultures and historical periods that produce them, and then they gradually lose their significance. The standards of Roman armies with their inscription "SPQR" no longer arouse more than esoteric historic interest. Nor does the symbolism of the dream dances of the indigenous people of Australia's Outback speak to tourist audiences with the meaning it has for the dancers themselves. But there is a certain dimension of some symbols that seem to have impact that can to some extent be felt universally.

At the root of this timeless and worldwide symbolizing lies the fact that, despite the seemingly total diversity of humans' experience because of cultural differences, there is some community of human experience. Cultures may understand very differently such experiences as birth and death. They may interpret their meaning in almost contradictory fashion, but all humans are born and all humans die. Both events are mysterious, and both require people to interpret them. Both events in themselves are symbolic in depth beyond any particular interpretation. Even though the explanations and rituals connected with these events can be so different from one culture to another, when persons in one culture are exposed to the very different interpretative symbols of another culture they can still resonate with the underlying shared meaning of death, and this can give them insight into the unfamiliar symbols of the other culture. Thus, the basic sequence of humans' lives—birth, growth, maturation, human relations, success or failure, suffering, aging, and death—no matter how differently understood and experienced, has a level of intrinsic meaning for all humans, a radical symbolism that all humans can share.

It is because of this "community of experience" that great literature or art produced in one culture can be appreciated by another culture or historical period. Though the precise interpretation of that literature will inevitably be different, there is a certain universality of "the human" that artistic genius grasps and to which it pays symbolic tribute. Perhaps at the root of this phenomenon is the fact that human life in its essential reality is mystery, and though the attempts to understand and express that mystery by true art or philosophical reflection is always revelatory, the full extent of that mystery always escapes any symbolizing. Life cannot be completely understood; it can only be lived.

Around these "common" experiences, there accumulate symbolisms that can be appreciated universally. For example, the experience of a storm that threatens injury or death can give storms a symbolic meaning of danger—so the symbolism in the movie *The Perfect Storm*. But the meaning of water—in the movie, wild stormy water capable of destroying life—can be multiple. Water can also be experienced as soothing pain, stimulating plant life, or assuaging thirst. These various experiences of water can be imagined, perhaps triggered by pictures of a desert or fields being irrigated. It may be that one remembers a past experience or hears someone recalling a memory and so shares vicariously in this remembered experience. In any case, the imagination or memory has the power to carry meaning, arouse emotion, and influence action. Modern psychiatry has made us aware of the power of remembered experiences, even when these are suppressed.

Function of Symbols

When one is dealing with these key human experiences, because they are always mysterious and even perplexing, one turns to metaphor as a vehicle of insight. Some of the "springboard" of the metaphor is supplied by nature itself, by the bodily perceptions connected with the event—for example, smoke for fire. In other instances, poetic insight discovers a deep existential link of one thing with another, so that the beauty of a rose can give one insight into the beauty of a beloved friend (unless your friend is the hopeless scientist described above). In still other cases, a purely arbitrary social decision establishes an artificial linkage between two things—for example, the United States and an eagle. Customary usage leads to the experience of an eagle making one think about this nation. A particular item, the bald eagle, can become a "classic" symbol of the United States.

There are also "accidental" events such as a war that are experienced by a group and where a group meaning emerges. This also can find symbolic expression in, for example, the marines raising the flag at Iwo Jima. Families, too, have such special happenings, as well as pictures or other memorabilia that continue to trigger memory of that happening, and these serve to strengthen the identity and unity of the family.

Symbols, then, perform several different functions on several different levels. On the simplest level, there are mere signs. An image or sound is arbitrarily chosen to represent some message. The usual example of a pure sign is a stop sign. Red, octagonal signs with white lettering usually mean to cease movement. Period. An "exit" sign means only that—this way out. Our lives are full of such signs and very helpful they are, indeed. Some signs, however, acquire a far deeper meaning. As we described above, these touch our very existence and help to shape it. Some symbols seem to be nearly universal—for instance, flowers as a sign of beauty (except, it seems, for your beloved scientist, sigh). Some symbols are particular to some societies: white dresses for brides is very much a western European custom. Still others are specific to countries, like the bald eagle mentioned above, which speaks volumes to citizens of the United States. There are some symbols that are limited to certain families and even individuals, although the most powerful symbols are usually shared by a wider group.

Interestingly, however, you might notice that one person's sign might be another person's symbol. Some drivers don't see stop signs as just signs, for example. They are a challenge, or an affront, and they call up deep feelings and sometimes unexpected acceleration. Different countries understand stop signs in different ways as well. A friend of mine rented a car in Rome and was driving through town when he stopped for a stop sign. He was immediately rear-ended. The furious motorist who had struck him raced up and demanded what the hell he was doing. My friend meekly pointed to the stop sign and said, "I was stopping, of course." "Stop," the irate Roman roared, "not park!" In Rome, it would seem, stop signs mean slow down (slightly).

Signs always have the potential to become symbols, and even the most powerful symbols can lose their force as time passes and society changes. The world of signification is a constantly fluid one, living and vibrant. This very human world shapes us in many ways, and it is important to understand how they do so and what problems the power of symbols create for those who study them.

Rituals have been analyzed and dissected by scholars for centuries, and debates have raged over exactly how to describe rituals and what counts as a ritual. For the sake of this book, we will use a simple definition: a ritual is a symbol that is acted out. All rituals are symbols, therefore, but not all symbols are rituals. The long-stemmed red roses given to a loved one are a symbol. Getting down on one knee in an expensive restaurant and presenting your beloved with one perfect rose as a prelude to a proposal of marriage is a ritual (although your lovely scientist might not get it). As we will see later, the Latin word used in Western Christianity for centuries, *sacramentum*, can mean both symbol and ritual. Thus the title of this book is *Christian Symbol and Ritual: An Introduction*, even though most of the book deals with those symbols that are acted out—that is, rituals.

Symbolism and Interpretations of Experience

One of the principal characteristics of the turn toward critical thinking that has marked modern times has been the realization that people's assumption of the obvious realism of daily perception is not as well founded as we had presumed. We do not really see things simply as they are; we see them *as we see them*. Our previous understandings, our fears and desires, our education, our expectations: all feed into our perception.

Perception is not a mirroring of that which we perceive, though ordinary "common sense" often takes that for granted. Instead, it involves a double becoming. I as a knower, *become the object* of which I am aware. It speaks to me, and I must try to be as open a listener as possible. In my consciousness of that object it *becomes a "known"*—that is, it exists intentionally as well as extra-mentally. Because it functions as a word to me, the known object or happening carries—as do spoken words—a certain meaning, a meaning that has been for the most part shaped prior to my experience by the language (my mother tongue) that has given shape to my thinking processes.

For example, I know that a tree that exists quite apart from my knowing it. I can even surmise that if the tree falls in the forest, the underbrush will be crushed. However, it is also true that I only know trees as I know them with all the overtones that trees have for me. Maybe I always associate trees with wonderful family camping trips. Maybe I associate trees with ecology and so see trees as a symbol of a natural world to be preserved. A scientist might see a tree as a factory for producing oxygen. However you understand trees, that understanding entails an "intentional understanding"—all the human feeling and attributions we bring with us to trees. Even our senses are human senses. Who knows how a squirrel senses a "tree" or what a "tree" is for a squirrel?

Certainly it is not the same as for a human. Few of us live in trees and store our food there. So the old question: Would that tree make a sound if it fell in the forest and no human was around? Since "sound" is something human (as opposed to whatever noise animals sense), you could say there is no sound.

Happenings, above all happenings to me, are even more subject to the vagaries of perception. That is why three people who witness the same happening—for example, an automobile accident—often given three quite different accounts of what happened. No two events are ever exactly the same; yet, we tend to interpret a particular event by putting it into an already existent category. The driver of one of the cars involved in a crash emerges from his car and walks rather unsteadily alongside his car, and we observe him as a drunken driver when actually he may simply be dazed from the collision. What really is the "word" that a particular person I encounter or a particular event I experience "speaking" to me? What is the meaning to which I must try to listen in the myriad happenings of life?

Another way of saying this is that for me as a person, a conscious being, the most important aspect of the things that enter into my perception of the world around me, as well as the perception of myself, is the meaning these things have for me. Most of them may have little meaning, so I scarcely notice them and certainly don't remember them for any length of time. Every now and then something significant, meaningful, does happen, and so it draws my attention, perhaps elicits some response from me. If it is "remark-able," I do remark on it with several of those I meet that day, or even recall it for several days in the future. It may well be that several of those to whom I speak about it respond with very little enthusiasm because for them it is not significant: it does not carry the same meaning that it does for me.

The externals of my perceptions—what I see and hear and feel and smell—lead me in terms of my conditioning to the deeper reality beneath them. They are "words," or to use a more common designation of them, the *signs and symbols* discussed above. In many instances, I do not admit to the fact that a certain combination of observed size and color and shape function as signs to tell me that I am seeing a dog. I just take that for granted. Smoke and flames pouring from a window let me know that there is a fire; what I directly observe is smoke and flames, but what I experience is a fire.

Clearly, symbolism functions in all our knowing, even in what seems most immediate and direct. However, as we will see, there are symbols and then there are *symbols*. It will take each of us a lifetime to learn just a bit of the way to interpret and use them, but upon our ability to do so will depend our self-identity, our successes or failures, our happiness.

Language, Basic Symbol System

One of the benefits of the past few decades has been the careful study of symbolism, especially of the most basic symbol system, which is language. These studies indicate that our world is not so much a "real world out there" as an intentional world, a world created out of our experiences not only as minds but also as bodies. Symbols and particularly language determine to a large extent how we organize the world. Symbol and language, moreover, are communal by nature. A word known only by one person is useless; a symbol practiced by only one person communicates nothing.

Therefore we are born into a world already shaped by language and by symbol; in fact, this world is created by language and symbol. Moreover, this humanly created world precedes us. Children are constantly being trained to understand these symbols and this language so they can operate and communicate successfully in the world their culture has created around them. Most basically, children need to be taught to "see" the world. As studies by Jean Piaget (1896–1980) the Swiss anthropologist demonstrate, children even need to learn such simple skills as depth perception.

Rituals train us to see the world in a certain way. Beds, chairs, and sofas are not trampolines; knives, forks, and spoons should convey food to our mouths, they are not be used as weapons against our siblings. Children do not automatically or naturally know these things, they must be taught. Most of that teaching occurs by ritual: by watching others perform the ritual and by imitating them. By saluting the flag, kneeling down in church, sitting (relatively) quietly in a classroom while the teacher is speaking, by simply dressing a certain way each morning (you don't wear swimming trunks to work as a bank teller), we re-create a world that we have been trained to re-create. In fact, we re-create that world so thoroughly that it becomes second nature to us; we cease to see it as created and start to see it as natural.

Language, too, shapes us. Each language presumes a worldview as any student of a new language can tell you. *Perro, chien,* and *Hund* are all words that refer to the same creature, but there are overtones to the English word, "dog," that none of these other words can carry. Only the English "dog" spelled backward becomes the word for divinity, for example, and therefore can be used for subtle jokes. The French expression *entre chien et loup* doesn't mean anything to English speakers even if translated (what English speaker would ever guess that "between the dog and the wolf" refers to dusk). People who call some furry, four-legged animals "dogs" see the world slightly differently then those who call them *chiens.* In fact, because of this (and all the other of millions of words that make up a language), the "world" they see is actually different for those who pat a *chien* on the head (*sur la tête*) and those who *darle palmaditas al perro en la cabeza* (which isn't quite the same thing at all). According to Richard Hale, the linguist who taught for many years at MIT, "When you lose a language, you lose a culture, intellectual wealth, a work of art. It's like dropping a bomb on a museum, the Louvre."[2]

2. Richard Hale, quoted in the *Economist* (November 3–9, 2001): 89.

I

Characteristics and Functions of Rituals

Problems in Understanding Symbols and Rituals

As is probably clear by now, symbols and rituals can mean different things to different people. Surely the flag of the United States stirs up very different emotions in a citizen of the United States than in citizens of other countries, particularly those people who oppose the foreign policy of the United States. For the former, it is a sacred symbol of freedom and democracy. For the latter, it can be the symbol of an oppressive and intolerant regime.

This problem becomes a more acute problem for those scholars who study the symbols and rituals of other people. How can someone from the outside appreciate and understand the symbols and rituals of another people? If a scholar remains dispassionate and "objective," just reporting what ritual objects look like and how they are used in a ceremony, the feeling and power of the ritual is lost. If a scholar then adds some description of the meaning the ritual has for those involved, the implication may well be that this is somehow "not real." Maybe those who use the symbol or practice the ritual think and feel it has power, but "in fact" (that is, for the scholar) it does not. If the scholar goes further and joins in the ritual as a participant, feeling the effect of the ritual as a true participant, then the scholar loses her or his "objectivity"—that is, it becomes harder to describe that ritual in a way that will be meaningful for other scholars.

Insiders and Outsiders

Either one is an "insider" (that is, a participant), or one is an "outsider" (that is, an observer). If one is an insider, one experiences as real the emotion and the effect of the ritual; if one is an outsider, one can better evaluate how the ritual shapes the culture of the individuals involved and even whether the ritual actually performs what it is meant to perform. Who then can better describe the ritual involved? Certainly only an insider can describe the effect the ritual has on her or his life, while the outsider is much better situated to describe how a ritual fits into a pattern shared by rituals of other cultures or how a ritual reflects the power structure and organization of a society.

The inevitable question then arises: Which one of the two is "right?" Which one describes the truth of the ritual? There appears to be no adequate answer to this question, since both the insider and the outsider are speaking from particular cultural stances. For the insider, the ritual reflects reality; what the ritual promises, it delivers (under the proper circumstances). But if you read carefully, you will notice that "outsiders" in this discussion refers to academics, scholars who study other cultures. Scholars also have a culture with its own worldview and its own rituals. When scholars are in their world and perform their rituals, they are "insiders" and have the same problems as other "insiders." In short, everyone is an "insider" in her or his own world, and everyone belongs to some world or other. There is no one who is an "outsider" to all worlds; there is no one who is truly "objective."

So, once again, are the rituals of a particular group "real"? Do they do what they intend to do? Well, that depends. "Insiders" might say yes about the very same ritual that some "outsiders" would say no. When "insiders" and "outsiders" disagree, they have to then start to compare the differences in their worldviews that lead them to different ways of understanding the rituals in question. This sort of mutual and respectful discussion of differences in worldviews is a real opportunity for both people involved to learn and grow, but it is possible—and even likely—that no "objective" answer to the question of the "reality" of the ritual will be reached. We will see later how this insight into insiders and outsiders can help answer questions about Christian rituals: questions, for instance, about the "real" presence of the risen Christ in the Christian meal. For now, it is enough to notice that one must judge others from inside their own culture and that everyone lives in a particular culture with its own rituals.

Rituals and Power

Rituals not only celebrate the deepest values of a culture, they also create, maintain, and legitimize that culture. Part of the process of legitimization necessarily entails the negotiation of power within a society, so that important rituals and symbols in every society are essential for maintaining the power structures of that society. State banquets, for instance, are often a diplomatic nightmare, since the relative worth of each country to the host determines the position of the representatives of various countries at the table. Individual ambassadors, of course, may not agree with their placement; they may be insulted by it. Even in a family, the positions at the table of the head of the family, of visitors, and of children are determined by their roles in the family. Graduation from the "kiddy" table to the "adult" table at Thanksgiving can be a major moment in the life of a young adult. Hence, the wisdom of the legendary "round table" of King Arthur: the knights were symbolically equal, with no head or foot of the table.

This is not to imply that rituals necessarily or automatically somehow "force" a particular power structure on an unwilling minority. Rituals are more complex than that. By consent to the ritual, in fact, those not in positions of power not only acquiesce to the power structure but also actually create and maintain that structure. Their agreement is itself an act of power without which the ritual ceases to be effective. Rituals and symbols, then, more accurately *negotiate* power within a group or society. For this very reason, they are often open to a broad interpretation that is acceptable to disparate groups within the larger society that practices the ritual.

When hundreds of people gather to watch fireworks for the Fourth of July, for example, all certainly agree that they are celebrating the founding of the United States as a country and are proud to be "Americans." Some, though, think immediately of the United States as a military power and almost exclusively identify this holiday with the military. Others would see the military as marginal to the holiday that for them celebrates the individual rights and liberties upon which the nation was founded. Still others understand the celebration to represent the country's openness over the centuries to immigrants fleeing oppression or economic hardship. The ambiguity of the symbol allows everyone to enjoy the fireworks and celebrate being a citizen without agreeing about what exactly being a "100 percent American" entails.

Rituals and symbols constantly create and re-create power structures within a society by continuously negotiating the legitimizing of power within the group or society. On the one hand, leaders of the rituals certainly lead because they have power, and the rituals constantly remind others of their power. On the other hand, participants in rituals by their continued participation grant that power to the leaders. If and when participants no longer participate in the ritual or acquiesce to the leadership in the ritual, then the leadership simply ceases being leaders. Rituals and symbols, therefore, have to continually meet the needs both of the dominant group of leaders and of several minority constituencies. When this negotiation fails, new patterns of leadership emerge.

Power and Christian Rituals

Christian rituals are no exception to this dynamic. Down through the centuries, Christian rituals and symbols have been in a constant state of negotiation between clergy and laity, dominant cultures and minority cultures. When the rituals have successfully balanced these concerns, they have been accepted as central to Christianity. When they have not, they have either successfully negotiated a new power relationship or slowly withered away. In the early Middle Ages, for instance, kings, queens, emperors, and empresses were considered to be ordained clergy, performing an important role in the hierarchy of the Christian church. However, over several centuries, the Christian community, particularly in western Europe, redefined leadership roles within the church, and royalty slowly ceased being accepted as clergy. The ritual of coronation ceased being also an ordination. The community had renegotiated the constitution of its leadership.

The issue of power becomes of particular moment when discussing religious rituals, since those rituals are often understood to be one means of communicating the divine presence to the community. Certainly this is true of Christianity. If the rituals depend on certain leadership roles, those roles (as opposed to the rituals) may eventually come to be seen to mediate the divine. The more the community understands the divine to be mediated mainly or even exclusively through rituals, the more important the leadership roles in those rituals become. In extreme cases, these roles may become identified with the divine so completely that the leadership is understood to stand in the place of God. On the whole, Christianity has resisted this extreme, but the discussion of the role of ritual as negotiating social power is very helpful in understanding how leadership in the Christian community developed over the centuries. To some extent, it also helps explain the many divisions within Christianity.

For now, let it suffice to say that Christian symbols and rituals are not immune to the ordinary social processes that shape other symbols and rituals in human society. Symbols and rituals create, shape, and re-create societies in a constant renegotiation of power. Symbols and rituals can be said in the truest sense to make and to break the societies in which they function.

Ambiguity in Symbols

In general, Western society prizes "clear and distinct ideas." We like things to be what they are and only what they are. "So," students often ask after a long rehearsal of the different stands scholars take on an issue, "Who's right? Which of these people is describing what is really going on?" It is immensely frustrating for them if not only the professor doesn't know, but also, at the moment, no one seems to know. The world, many students (and others) think, is stable, straightforward, and clear. If the professor doesn't give one clear answer to their questions, it's because she or he is either stupid or being deliberately difficult. Usually professors have to settle for the (somewhat) easier answer to the question "What will be on the exam?"

Much of human life, however, is not "clear and distinct"—and certainly not symbols and rituals (apart, perhaps, from some signs as described above). That is why, as mentioned above, people attending the same ritual often experience it differently. Symbols are polyvalent: that is, they carry several meanings at the same time. They are also "ambiguous," in the sense that the scholar Susan Ross describes them in her book on Christian rituals, *Extravagant Affections: A Feminist Sacramental Theology.*

According to Ross, Christian symbols and rituals are more amorphous, more slippery—more human, if you will—than most Christian insider descriptions of those rituals and symbols allow. When and where, for instance, is the risen Christ present in the community—only in the reading of scripture; only when the properly appointed minister says so; only in the consecrated bread and wine; only within our group? Which rituals really carry that presence—only those approved by the leadership of Christianity; in all gatherings of Christians to share their faith; in home altars; in roadside shrines? Or are there different "levels of presence" in different rituals? Is the risen Christ "more" present at a Roman Catholic Mass than in a family sharing a meal at the grave of a loved one on the anniversary of her or his death?

There is a Christian theology that tries very hard to nail down "clear and distinct" answers to the above questions. One twelfth-century theologian in Paris even tried to work out how far away a priest could be from the bread for the words of consecration to change the bread into the body of Christ (halfway down the aisle of the church; all the way down; out the door?). Ross would suggest that Christian symbols and rituals simply don't work this way. First of all, it would be arrogant (and very dangerous) to decide for God how God will be experienced in human life. It would be nice if God were at our beck and call, but then, if God were, God wouldn't be what most Christians call God. Further, some Christians experience the presence of the risen Christ much more fully in rituals and symbols that are not "official" and, in fact, find that presence lacking in some "official" rituals. The divisions between "official" and "unofficial" rituals (to use one form of insider language, between "sacraments" and "sacramentals"), the divisions between leadership and followers (again, in insider language, between clergy and laity) are amorphous, both historically and personally. As we shall see, what counts as "official" changes over the course of Christian history, as does the understanding of who is an "official" leader. Moreover, there are certainly communities in which unofficial ceremonies and unofficial leaders carry far more importance than the official ones. It is important to keep this in mind as we investigate individual Christian practice.

Rituals as Unique

One further point needs to be made about rituals. Real rituals are never generic, never repeatable, and never exist in books. Nothing in this book is a ritual (except maybe the ways in which you read it). Rituals only occur to real people at real times in real places. This may seem too obvious to mention, but sometimes people think rituals are contained in books of rituals or descriptions of a ritual someone attended. These aren't rituals at all, just guides for possible future rituals.

For example, imagine the difference between your high school graduation and some movie or book about a graduation or graduations in general. There's no comparison. The books or movies don't have the people you know with all the loves and hates that entails. They can't even begin to describe your own experience of hope and loss and fear and excitement. They can't have your dress or your suit, your cap and gown with you in it. And that event will never be repeated, even if you could fit into that dress again or button up those pants. You will never be the same you who walked down that aisle, grabbed that diploma, and perhaps tripped going down the stairs. Even your memories of that event are not the event. Every single ritual that ever happened or ever will happen is, was, or will be unique.

Rituals of Growing Up

Humans comprise such a diverse group that it is hard to state with certainty that all cultures share certain experiences, much less certain rituals. Nevertheless, there are some actions that all humans share. All of us humans are born into a particular society. We all start out as children and gradually become adults. In order for that to happen, we have to eat at regular intervals. Upon becoming an adult, we take up positions in our respective societies. We form friendships and come together to procreate. In some societies, these two activities are understood to be linked; in others not. People need some way to negotiate misunderstandings. Many undergo illness and, at least so far, all die.

This may seem pretty basic, but these common experiences are also very powerful. Not surprisingly, humans symbolize and ritualize all these acts, although in very different ways. Before looking at the way in which Christians specifically address these key moments in every human life, it might be helpful to first look at how societies in general celebrate the key activities of human existence.

There are many ways of approaching the varied, ever changing, and colorful dance of life which makes up rituals, but for the purpose of our study, we will organize everyday rituals into the larger pattern of growing up.

Linking all the experiences and their meanings, important or banal, is the underlying sequence of every day experience that we call "our life." For each of us, that has been and continues to be a process of growing up: of developing (hopefully) a more balanced, mature, and accurate view of ourselves and of the world in which we live. Another way of naming this years-long journey toward adulthood is "socialization." Our becoming who we are takes place within a network of relationships—within our family, then our neighborhood and human environment, our peer group and friends, and then perhaps within the broader context of the country in which we live. We become who and what we are by reacting with the worldview and values of the culture that is ours—in some instances absorbing and agreeing with that culture, in others perhaps reacting against what we consider inadequate or false elements of that culture.

Stages of Maturation

For each individual, the process of maturation is somewhat distinctive. Not in every case is there a true movement toward maturity. Many people seem to never grow up. However, the ideal is a growth pattern that has been studied by developmental psychologists where there are identifiable steps that mark most people's advance toward mature adulthood. Depending on the historical period when one lives and the cultural context in which life unfolds, there may be quite distinctive patterns of growth. Not too long ago in a culture like the United States a person passed from infancy into childhood, then at about age fifteen into the beginnings of adult responsibility and employment, then in the early twenties into founding a family and full adult responsibility, then at about age fifty-five into growing old and retirement, and finally at about age sixty-five into preparation for death. Today there are several additional "steps of passage": one goes from childhood into puberty and then adolescence, then early adulthood with full adult responsibility coming at roughly age thirty, then full adult years followed by middle age and retirement, and after seventy or so old age, with death often coming in the eighties or nineties. This means that there are more "passages," each with its specific meaning and requiring some adjustment in activity and outlook.

As a person experiences this process of growing up, there is an unfolding of life's meaning, acceptance or rejection of what is perceived as that meaning, and acceptance or rejection or choice of an unfolding self-identity. Life is not a given. Particularly in a rapidly changing world, life is a journey, often unexpected and uncertain and often without a road map.

To aid people to find their way on this journey, to find the meaning their life has and should have and how to achieve that meaning, society structures a pattern of education. This begins with parents instructing and guiding their children; is furthered by formal schooling where children are socialized into the world beyond their homes; and is then continued in different ways depending on people's occupations, interests, and social involvements.

Discovering and celebrating the meaning of the various stages in this process of growing up has traditionally been aided by people gathering for rituals. Families in wealthy industrialized societies, for instance, celebrate together the arrival of a child in the family, the beginning of a child's entry into school, passage from grade school to high school and maybe then to college, graduations from high school and possibly college, promotions in a job, engagements and marriages, success in a career, and so on. All societies seem to have birth rituals and at least some rituals to mark the transition from childhood to adulthood, even if this passage sometimes lacks the succession of stages that occur in industrialized societies. Such celebrations express what a group of people thinks is the meaning of their lives and what will be the meaning of the years ahead. These celebrations are occasions when people ritualize their understanding of who and what they are and share their commitment to finding and creating together a meaning for their lives. Ritual actions are important ways in which people grow together as a society. In the educational process, young persons are taught the ways to interpret more accurately the meaning of these rituals and of themselves. If the rituals truly function as rituals and do not become sheer routine repetition of familiar civic or religious practices, they themselves carry on throughout people's lives the function of making life meaningful.

The entrance of a person into the society is an obvious occasion for celebration and, more importantly, can be seen as a process whereby a person is accepted and then reaccepted and repositioned within the society throughout their life. Birth is the first such occasion since a person never just appears on earth as a fully independent individual; she or he appears within a family and a society that welcomes her or him (gratefully or not), celebrates the continuation of their society, and begins immediately to celebrate the new role of the parents in that society. Celebrations around the birth of a child are not, for obvious reasons, directed exclusively or even mainly at the baby who cannot at that stage understand much of the fuss that is made around them. The celebrations more clearly welcome the parents into a new position in society. They are now no longer the children, but the parents. They have become something new, and their new status deserves recognition and support by the community. These celebrations mark a twofold welcoming: the welcoming of the child into the society, and the initiation of the parents into a new role within the society. Hopefully, the societal celebrations mark a new level of maturation for the parents and a more serious level of commitment to the society as the caretakers of the future of that society.

Of course, people can enter societies in other ways than being born into them. Rituals mark the entrance of immigrants into citizenship when a person solemnly swears to uphold the values of her or his new home. Graduation ceremonies are a clear demarcation between the different stages of educational and profession states. Most societies have very important celebrations that accompany the entrance of children into adulthood. These include the formal religious ceremonies of a bar mitzvah or bat mitzvah, as well as the less formal ceremonies of the high school senior prom. Most groups—Boy Scouts, Girl Scouts, Masons, Rotary, fraternities and sororities, and even neighborhood clubs—have initiation ceremonies marking the entrance of new members into fellowship or sisterhood. A constant round of initiatory ceremonies accompanies each life as a person moves into new roles in society and thus renegotiates her or his relationship to that society.

Rituals and Power Structures

Rituals mark the many stages of maturation within groups and societies. Rituals also delineate the power structures within a group or society. The president of the United States is not president until he or she undergoes an inauguration ceremony. A Christian bishop is not considered a bishop until she or he undergoes a consecration. Some sort of ceremony of this kind marks most leadership roles, although not all such ceremonies actually enact what they ritualize. In ancient Roman society the move to a new rank or role in society—that is, to a new *ordo*—was marked by a ceremony called an *ordinatio*. In our society, most groups from governments to churches "ordain" their leaders in a ceremony that marks their entrance into a new level of responsibility and service to the community.

Such ceremonies tell society "who's who": who gets to do what, and who has to obey whom. Not only are such roles marked by an initiation ceremony, but also most offices are marked by symbols demonstrating one's rank. Judges wear robes; police have distinctive uniforms, and academics have their gowns. Such symbols can only be worn by those empowered by the group to wear them. In ancient Roman society, it would have been illegal to wear the robes of another rank, and, even today, to wear a police uniform without actually being a police officer can get you in real legal trouble.

Rituals of Friendship and Marriage

Humans not only ritualize the taking on of new leadership roles but also celebrate new relationships between individuals. Two striking examples of this are friendship rituals and marriage. In many societies the two have become almost synonymous.

Marriage, for much of human history and in many societies today, is an arrangement between families for the continuation and betterment of the two families involved. The marriage ceremony celebrates the union of the two families in hopes that offspring will result to carry on the good name and fortune of the two families involved. One thing marriage is not is necessarily a personal relationship. You may hopefully get to like and perhaps even love your spouse, but that is not really the point of marriage. Marriage, in this sense, is a union of two families, witnessed by and accepted by the larger community, for the purposes of procreation and enrichment. It is a very public act, an act of the community. In fact, it is most fundamentally the act that celebrates the continuation of the community: the hope that the community will continue in a future generation.

Friendship, in contrast, is most centrally between individuals. Friendship recognizes a kinship between two people, the acceptance to a greater or lesser extent of a mutual regard and admiration. In most periods in Western societies, it was friendship, not marriage, that embodied love. Ancient and medieval writers in the West sang the praises of friendship as true and everlasting loyalty. One would do anything for one's friend, even give up one's own life. True friendship and the loyalty that entailed were considered one of the greatest goals of human life.

Not surprisingly, rituals existed and still exist to celebrate such a relationship. Some languages even differentiate between "you" who are my friend, and "you" who are everybody else. There is a big difference between *tu* (the informal, friendly "you") in French and *vous* (the formal "you"), and it is important not to confuse the two. Many friendship rituals are personal and private, but others are more public. Among some German speakers, one more or less formally celebrates the moment when one is called *du* (the friendly "you") and no longer *Sie* (the formal "you").

Even in early Hebrew society, however, as we shall see, there are indications that many people did hope that marriage would be based on a deep friendship and even expected that kind of friendship to occur. Many Christian writers seem to understand such a friendship and love as not simply fundamental to a marriage but even as a powerful symbol of the deep friendship and love that exists between God and humans. Gradually, in a process not yet clear to historians, the understanding of marriage as basically a friendship came to overshadow the understanding of marriage as an alliance between families. In our society, the two relationships of marriage and friendship have to a large extent merged. One is expected to marry one's closest friend for precisely the reason that he or she is your friend, the one you love. This means that the meaning attached to the rituals and symbols of marriage now also carry the meaning that rituals of friendship once did. However, the wedding ceremony did not abandon the rituals attached to marriage as a union of two families, and many laws governing marriage hark back to this earlier understanding of marriage. Add to this the fact that some people hold, on one level or other, both understandings of marriage, and a good deal of confusion can result. Is a wedding fundamentally something the family celebrates, or is it fundamentally a personal ceremony between two friends? Can two people of the same sex who are best friends marry, or is marriage fundamentally for procreation? The relationship between marriage and friendship is still being negotiated in our society, and so it should come as no surprise that the debates over who can or cannot celebrate a valid wedding ritual remain a heated issue.

Ritual Meals

Meals should always be celebrations, and for many societies, always are. About this there is little debate, heated or otherwise. People rarely just graze or gulp. They dine; they talk; they sip; they savor. One could argue that true dining is truly being human. Few people, except from necessity, do not somehow relish the nourishment they receive, even if it is only to spend some time in preparation. Cooking, spicing, roasting, baking all are processes not just of making raw materials palatable—they are ceremonies that make food presentable, attractive, interesting: in short, human. The German language wisely separated what animals do with food (*fressen*) and what humans do (*essen*). The difference, at least from the point of view of this book, would be that rituals make *essen* more than mere *fressen*.

Meals are also essentially communal actions. To really enjoy a meal, conversation and companionship are necessary. Especially at specifically ritual meals, from "family nights" to Thanksgiving to important ritual meals like the Jewish Seder or the Christian Eucharist, meals also determine and establish who comprise our friends, family, and community. The meals, more or less formally, establish the community. Eating, and more importantly, refusing to eat with people, is central in establishing who is or is not a member of our group. In many societies, to invite a person to your table involves serious obligations of hospitality. Refusal to allow someone to eat with you would equally be an insult in most societies. Eating with others in most human circles entails both privileges and responsibilities that must be taken seriously.

The placement at meals establishes, reinforces, and constantly renegotiates power structures with the group that eats together. As mentioned above, those who arrange state dinners must carefully determine the placement of ambassadors. As every mother of the bride knows, the seating arrangements at a wedding can be more treacherous an endeavor than the most delicate international peace negotiations. Families customarily place the head of the family at the head of the table. Here, too, meals have an important role in the process of maturation. Moving to the head of the table, having the festive meals at your house rather than your parents' or siblings' houses—all these are as clearly ritual celebrations of coming into a new leadership role in the family as would be sitting at the head of a important international gathering.

Meals are not limited, either, to the living. Most societies celebrate meals in memory of the dead, even sharing their meal with the members of their community who are no longer physically present. Food is shared with saints, with ancestors, and in meals like Thanksgiving, in memory of those who have sacrificed for the welfare of the community. Such meals are extraordinarily powerful, for those who are commemorated are often considered really present and really part of the communal meal. In societies where such rituals are frequent and important, those no longer physically present are as much alive and part of the community as the living.

Rituals for Death and Dying

The celebration of the continued presence of the dead at the community's ritual meals is only one way that humans deal with death. All human groups must inevitably come to terms with the fact of death, even if that accommodation is to do one's best to deny and ignore it. Many societies do much more than this, however. Many rituals are directed at somehow helping the dying in what is understood as just another event in a person's life. Death is, if you will, the final stage of the maturation process. By aiding the person through the offering of prayers for their salvation, or by providing them with the necessities for the afterlife, the bond is maintained between the community and those members who have entered this new stage of existence.

The rituals surrounding death, however, are not just to accommodate the dead person. Such rituals are also meant to comfort and reassure the living. The communities, such rituals assert, continue despite the changed status of the dead person within that community. Remembrance of the dead reassures the living that they, too, will be remembered and be included as part of the community when they face their own death. Most fundamentally, the rituals and symbols surrounding death reassure the living that death has meaning and therefore death cannot negate the meaning of life.

Rituals for Healing

Closely allied with the rituals and symbols surrounding death are those that negotiate the reminders of our inevitable mortality, illnesses. Here the community offers support to those in pain and fear. Rituals and symbols can reassure the ill that they are still valued members of the community and that they can count on the support of the community to help deal with their new situation, whether temporary or permanent. Of course, the rituals and symbols of some societies can send the opposite message, telling those who are ill that they are now marginalized, essentially invisible to the society or group. This can happen particularly in those societies that equally attempt to ignore death, since illness and old age are reminders of that of which they do not wish to be reminded.

Most societies understand the healing of illness as involving much more than just a kind of complicated plumbing, chemical, and electrical repair of the machine of the body. For these societies, healing must take place not only of the body but also of the person and of the society itself. Rituals are undertaken to restore balance and order to the person. Central here would be removal of guilt and the self-loathing that guilt can cause. When possible, peace is negotiated between the ill person and anyone she or he may have harmed. Closure of old wounds, from such a vantage point, involves much more than sutures. Illness is communal, and it is the community and the relations within that community that need constant healing. Rituals and symbols of forgiveness, of contrition, and of mutual acceptance become then as much part of healing as does physical recovery from physical disease.

Healing between communities is as important as healing within the community. Exploitation, domination, and the terrible violence of war are all societal illnesses that require rituals of healing, of sorrow, of contrition, and of forgiveness that need to take place over generations before any healing can take place. The first step in the process of healing occurs when one group publicly acknowledges a wrong done to another group. Some ritual action, say the laying of a wreath on a gravesite or the erection of a monument to the victims, may follow such an acknowledgement. Whenever groups wish to overcome past or present grievances, ritual gestures inevitably embody, celebrate, and commemorate that desire.

Rituals of healing, then, should also involve a process of maturation, a process that gradually acknowledges the limitations of our mortality. We get sick, we make horrible mistakes, we learn to forgive and be forgiven, we eventually die. At every stage of this process, symbolic acts and rituals accompany and embody the stages of development. Of course, one can merely mouth an apology and provide the accompanying ritual handshake. One can join in a ceremony of unity with past enemies with hatred still in one's heart. One can pray for the sick and yet not visit the elderly in one's own family. But these then are broken rituals—in Christian terms, sacrileges. Rituals are meant to embody the meaning they symbolize. When they don't, they are lies. Any ritual, any symbol, can be a lie, but it can only be a lie if it has an accepted meaning to begin with, a meaning that can be distorted.

Our purpose here has been to point out areas in which most societies have developed rituals and symbols that are meant to embody and accompany the process by which individuals accommodate to and fulfill themselves within a given society. Between birth and death lies a lifetime of new beginnings, new relationships of friendship, new possibilities of responsibility and leadership, countless opportunities to forgive and be forgiven, thousands of meals celebrating all these events. Our lifetimes are embodied, celebrated, and actualized in ritual and symbol. True, societies celebrate these events in a myriad of different ways to which such a short presentation cannot begin to do justice. Even using the English language limits and even belittles the richness of human symbol and ritual. Yet, it would seem, in one way or another, all humans are born, all eat, many have friends with whom they eat, many marry and have children, a few marry their friends, most get ill, some forgive and some are forgiven, all die. Most move from childhood to adulthood through a process of gradual maturation and growing responsibility, all within a community rife with symbols. Each stage of this lifelong process is marked with ceremony and ritual. Indeed, the ceremony and ritual of life make life human.

Christians, like all other humans, go through the same processes and therefore have their own rituals and ceremonies to celebrate the great moments in their lives. It is to these particular rituals and the understanding that Christians have of them that we now turn.

2

Rituals in the Christian Context

Every community of humans who share a symbolic world also share a language to describe that world. Much of this language is shared only, or mainly, by the community itself. Members of the community are "insiders" in the sense described in chapter one. Religions are no exception to this practice; they have their own traditional language that can confuse outsiders. Therefore, it might be useful to explain some of the insider language that Christians, as insiders, use when speaking of their rituals and symbols.

The problem is not just a straightforward one of translation, however. Religions claim to mediate the divine presence of God (or the gods) to humans. Not surprisingly, the rituals, the offices, and even the insider language used by religions can themselves be understood as sacred by their own religious communities. Christianity, for instance, particularly treasures a set of writings that were produced (roughly) in the first century after the death of Jesus, the central religious figure for Christians. These writings, combined with a larger number of books from earlier Jewish religious literature, are called simply *The Book* (Bible) and are considered sacred, inspired by God.

Sometimes even certain translations (or transliterations) of these writings, originally written in Hebrew or Greek, take on an aura of the sacred. The seventeenth-century use of "thee" and "thou," long abandoned in ordinary English usage, survives in some translations of the Bible, as if this once everyday usage had some special religious power. The Greek words *apostolos* (messenger), *discipolos* (student or follower), *episcopos* (supervisor), *presbyteros* (elder), and *diakonos* (servant) have been transliterated into the English words, "apostle," "disciple," "bishop," "priest," and "deacon" and in so doing cease being everyday words (as they were in Greek) and become insider words. These insider words take on a meaning that the Greeks never intended. Even the name of the great central religious figure of Christianity, Jesus Christ, is the Greek translation of his given name, Joshua (or Yeshua in Aramaic) and the title of Messiah given to him by his earliest followers. "Jesus Christ" is not so much the name of a person as a proclamation that Joshua is the Messiah. Most Christians are quite surprised when they learn this; they think of "Jesus Christ" as a name like "Joe Smith." It's not; it's insider language that has become so accepted that people have forgotten that it is such.

If even Christians as insiders don't always understand the origins of even the most important of their own insider language, outsiders are understandably sometimes lost when they hear Christians speak. This section of the book hopes to explain what Christians mean when they say things like, "Jesus Christ is the savior," or "Jesus Christ is risen," or centrally for this book, "Jesus founded the sacraments." Now, not all Christians agree on precisely what those affirmations entail, and no doubt some Christians will take issue with the explanations given below, but some kind of explanation of Christian insider language should help both non-Christians and Christians better understand the role rituals play in Christian communities.

Sacraments, Rituals, and Symbols

First, let us start with the word "ritual" itself. It is important to note that the earliest Christians never used the word "ritual." They never spoke English, so they couldn't. Greeks, Latins, Syrians, Copts, and Armenians (some of the earliest groups to become Christian) used different words for this phenomenon. In Latin, the word used most often for ritual and symbol was *sacramentum*, and Latin is the language that most influenced Christian insider language in western Europe. Because of this influence, there exists, at least for English speakers, not only the words "ritual" and "symbol" but also the interesting and theologically loaded insider word "sacrament" to refer to Christian rituals. While this term is clearly a transliteration of the Latin, it cannot, in fact, be translated back into the Latin as it would have been used by early or medieval Christian writers. There is no word in Latin from these periods that is the equivalent of the English word "sacrament" with its polemical overtones of Reformation and post-Reformation debates.

A few examples should suffice. When the great twelfth-century theologian Hugh of St. Victor wrote his monumental work *De sacramentis christianae fidei* [About the *sacramenta* of the Christian faith], he was not speaking of seven (or two or five) particular Christian rituals. He used the word *sacramentum* to refer to creation and redemption, as well all the rituals and symbols that preceded the birth of Jesus in periods of both natural law and Jewish law. The word as Hugh used it can mean something similar to the Greek *mysterion*, as well as symbol or ritual. Hugh also used *sacramentum* to describe individual Christian rituals, of course. As an example of one Christian *sacramentum*, Hugh gave the water that is used in baptism. Note that he did not give the ritual of baptism as an example, but just the water. Any thing, any action that God has used in the past, or now uses in the present, to sanctify humans is a *sacramentum*. The word is very difficult to translate. It means "ritual" or "symbol" surely, but only those rituals and symbols that sanctify. To transliterate the word as "sacrament," as the only English translation of Hugh's work does, is very misleading. In English, "sacrament" refers only to very specific formal Christian rituals, a far narrower meaning than Hugh ever intended. It would make little sense, for instance, in Hugh's understanding of *sacramentum* to argue about how many *sacramenta* there might be. Anything at all that mediates the divine presence to humans would be a *sacramentum* for Hugh and for other twelfth-century theologians.

The word *sacramentum* also appears in another and better-known medieval Christian writer, the Dominican friar, Tommaso d'Aquino or in his English name, Thomas Aquinas. According to Thomas, the *sacramentum* of the Eucharist consists of three elements: the *sacramentum tantum*, the *sacramentum et res*, and the *res tantum*. Consider the weird translations that result when every use of the word *sacramentum* by Thomas is translated by *sacrament* in English. Here is one popular translation of Thomas's explanation of the components of the Eucharist: "We can consider three things in this sacrament: namely, that which is sacrament only, and this is the bread and wine; that which is both reality and sacrament, to wit, Christ's true body; and lastly that which is reality only, namely the effect of this sacrament."[1] How many sacraments do we have in this one sacrament? Are sacraments then not reality? Are parts of the Eucharist not sacraments? The translation completely misses Thomas's point.

1. St. Thomas Aquinas, *Summa theologica*, vol. 2. Translated by the Fathers of the Dominican Province (New York: Benziger Brothers, 1947), 2438 (pars III, Q. 73, art. 6).

Let's try another translation without the English word sacrament at all: "We should consider three things in this ritual; namely that which is the symbol alone, and this is the bread and wine; that which is both the reality signified by that symbol and which is in turn itself a symbol, that is, Christ's true body; and lastly that which is the reality alone signified by the symbol, namely the effect of the ritual."

Sacramentum cannot mean sacrament here, or one loses the whole meaning of what Thomas is saying. The point being made here, and it was made over and over again by medieval theologians, is that bread and wine are symbols and even the real presence of the risen Christ is a symbol, a symbol of the unity in faith and love that make up the Christian community. The Eucharist both celebrates and empowers the faith and active love of the community.

Most importantly, the second translation demystifies the theology. We are no longer talking about some spiritual reality called "sacrament" that is different from ordinary human symbols and rituals. Indeed, it is precisely about human symbols and rituals (shared bread and wine) that Thomas and other medieval writers are talking. They use the same word, *sacramentum*, for Jewish and even pagan rituals and symbols. In short, any human symbol or ritual can be called a *sacramentum*; this is something one cannot say of "sacraments." We are now back in a human world which really can embody the divine in ordinary human actions.

The insider word, sacrament, then originally just meant any symbol or ritual that God chose to mediate salvation to humans. Basically, that's all that it still means. Yet, Christians have fought and still do fight bitterly over which rituals are "really" sacraments and how many Christian rituals there "really" are. Roman Catholics hold that there are seven sacraments. This is based on the late medieval practice that required that all students in theology to lecture on the *Book of Sentences* (or more exactly "Book of Excerpts" or "Book of Quotations") of the twelfth-century theologian Peter the Lombard. Peter had argued that there were seven central Christian rituals based on the practice of the time. There was a logic to this, as each of these rituals corresponded to important moments in the life of the faithful. In the sixteenth century, the reformers disagreed with this, arguing that the scriptures only referred to two, or maybe three, rituals as central to Christianity—that is, baptism, the Eucharist, and perhaps marriage. In any case, the communities split over this issue, and arguments were made on both sides as to whether Jesus had instituted seven, or two, or some other number of sacraments.

The debates seem a bit beside the point, given the original meaning of the word, and suggest that the fights are really over something else, which, of course, they are. When Christians argue that there are "really" only two sacraments (and no more) or that there are "really" seven sacraments (and no more), they mean that Jesus only instituted two or seven rituals that Christians can use. As is, we hope, clear from the preceding discussion, originally Christians did not think like that. A *sacramentum* (or *mysterion*, to use the even more inclusive Greek word) referred to any thing or action or person that mediated the presence of God to humans. Of course, the central person who mediates that presence for Christians is Jesus Christ (to use his Greek name and title), and it is to him that we now must turn.

Jesus as Symbol

Much of the significance of Christians' life experience and of the rituals they use to celebrate that experience are common to them and to non-Christians— for example, family meals and participation in civic holidays. But a range of rituals which, as noted above, are referred to as Christian sacraments are distinctive in their meaning and their effect. The ground of this distinctiveness is the symbolic impact of Jesus of Nazareth, of his person as well as of his life and dying and rising. So, an examination of this impact—which catechetically has been expressed by the phrase "sacraments were instituted by Christ"—is needed before we can go on to an examination of Christian rituals. To be sure, the fact that Christian rituals are of their nature recollections of Jesus, the Christ, demands that we understand clearly what it is that is recalled.

Bracketing for the moment a more accurate understanding of the manner in which Jesus can be said to have "instituted" sacraments, let us ask what it means to say that Jesus was a symbol. Roger Haight's recent book, *Jesus, Symbol of God*, has probed in depth this symbol dimension of Jesus, and the controversy over the book indicates that the notion is far from easy to grasp. Clearly, Jesus' use of symbolic language, especially his parables, which were narrative metaphors, introduces us to the symbolic dimension of his teaching. Faced, as were Israel's prophets before him, with the problem of communicating to others an understanding of a God who transcended any human images or ideas, Jesus turned, as they had, to language symbols and action symbols.

Earliest Christianity was very aware of Jesus' employment of symbols in his public career as a prophet. John's gospel, in particular, points to the symbolic aspect of Jesus' "miracles"; the word it uses to refer to Jesus' wonder works is "signs." When it narrates the scene of Jesus at the marriage feast in Cana changing water into wine, the gospel ends by saying, "This first of his signs Jesus did in Cana of Galilee" (John 2:11). Again, all the gospels record his curing of blindness and see it as a message to his opponents that he had the ability and was eager to cure their spiritual blindness.

Both Jesus himself and his early disciples were aware that such wonder works symbolized not only Jesus' own concern to heal but also the compassionate God who worked through Jesus and empowered him with the divine creative Spirit. That these "signs" of Jesus symbolized God's acting in and through Jesus needs to be understood in the deeper sense of symbol; these actions not only said that God, too, was compassionate; they said this because a compassionate God was actively present in Jesus' activity. The symbol "contained" the reality it spoke; Jesus' actions were God's actions.

More basic than the symbolizing of Jesus' teaching and wonder working was the symbolism of his everyday life as a Galilean Jew in the particular context of first-century Judaism. Because that fundamental human experience included for Jesus a constant awareness of God as his "Abba" (the familiar term in Aramaic for one's father; literally, "poppa"), and was transformed in its meaning by that awareness, it symbolized for Jesus himself the character of God as unconditionally loving. The significance of this is that it is in the ordinariness of everyday life that the God revealed in Jesus is revealed to all humans. If God is indeed a loving parent, evil does not have the last word in creation. God is constantly "on our side," protecting us but also challenging us to be our best; in short, loving us despite our shortcomings.

However, Christian faith makes a claim about the person and action of Jesus that gives an unparalleled depth to their symbolizing. Basic to Christian belief about Jesus is that he is the embodiment of God's own "Word." In John's Gospel and by later Christian writers, Jesus is described as the incarnation of that communicative dimension of God that created, and continues to create, energize, and enlighten humans. In the Greek, this dimension of God was called the *Logos*, often translated as "Word" in English. This would mean that the reality of symbol extends even to the divine level: God's self-communication is rooted in the mystery of the divine and eternal Word. It is this Word, functioning to communicate God's self-gift to humans, that is expressed in all creation but is uniquely embodied in Jesus. Jesus is God's self-communicating to humans, or as some contemporary scriptural scholars are expressing it, Jesus is God's parable. As Jesus, searching for words to describe God, turns to parables, God uses the "narrative" of Jesus' own person and career, to reveal self.

What occurred in Jesus and continues in his risen existence and activity as the Christ is unique to him, but because he is the paradigm of humanity, it is extended to all who do not refuse it. St. Paul expressed this by referring to believers as "adopted" and as sharing in the inheritance of Christ. Jesus himself is described in the gospel as saying, "No one knows the Son except the Father and no one knows the Father except the Son and anyone to whom the Son chooses to reveal him" (Matt. 11:27). The persons and lives of believers are meant to be, in their own way, "words" that symbolize the God revealed in Jesus. As we will see, it is this meaning of their lives that Christians bring to their participation in ritual.

Jesus' Death

While Jesus' entire life was meaningful for Christians, a special meaning is attached to his death. Every human death catches up the significance of all that has preceded it, but in Jesus' case there was added meaning. That meaning proved hard to grasp for his immediate disciples and for those to whom they preached the new gospel, however. If Jesus was God's anointed one, the Messiah, what sense did it make that he was executed as a condemned criminal? In response, those first Christians appealed to two prophetic texts. The first, Isaiah 52–53, describes a figure who, though innocent, would be unjustly put to death but in his death would save the people. The second text, Psalm 22, a Messianic psalm that begins with the words, "My God, my God, why have you forsaken me," describes God's chosen one in dying anguish, with pierced hands and feet, ravished by thirst, watching his executioners casting lots for his garments.

While those texts could, and did, place Jesus' death in the context of God's "use" of him as the source of human salvation, they express what is perhaps the most mysterious of spiritual ideals: suffering self-sacrifice for the sake of others. Moreover, they point to the underlying dynamic in Jesus' death: the conflict with evil (which gained momentum in his public career); the paradoxical defeat of evil even as evil forces were destroying Jesus' life; and the persisting power of God's Spirit that was made possible by Jesus' decision to remain faithful to his Abba, a power that then out of Jesus' dying created new human risen life.

Without question, the dying of Jesus, what was done to him and what he did as he died, has a symbolism of such density that Christian theology and contemplation have yet to explain it adequately. Death is the great enigma for humans. What meaning can it have when it represents the loss of everything people prize, when it inevitably challenges the best efforts of science and medicine, when its universality pays no respect to people's wealth or "importance"? Still, Christians believe that in a way yet not fully grasped, Jesus' dying reveals that out of death can come life. Death can have and should have meaning. No wonder, then, that Christian rituals recollect and ponder and celebrate that event.

Jesus' Resurrection

Still, Jesus' dying could not have the symbolic saving power it has if it were not for the prelude and source of the risen human life into which Jesus passed from death. It was the experience of Jesus alive again that opened up for Jesus' disciples a whole new and unexpected meaning of his life and death. Not only that; it meant that Jesus, now risen and become fully the Christ, was not absent from their lives. Instead, he was present to them and to all future history: "Remember, I am with you always, even to the end of the age" (Matt. 28:18). The symbolic impact of Jesus' resurrection is quite simple but incredibly profound: the very reality and meaning of death was transformed. All that death symbolized and still symbolizes for those without faith or hope in the God who "raised Jesus from the dead"—the ultimate threat and negation and evil to be feared—was rendered ineffective. Death was literally swallowed up in life.

Jesus, Savior

A fish was the ancient Christian symbol for their faith as Christians in Jesus as the Christ. This is well known today, and one finds the fish symbol on any number of automobiles. Why a fish? The first letters in the Greek words for "Jesus Christ Son of God Savior" (*Iesus christos theou uios soter*) spell out the word for "fish" (*icthus*). At a time when it was dangerous to be Christian, this secret symbol was used so that Christians could recognize one another as such.

What interests us in our discussion here is that Jesus was from the beginning seen as "savior." However, this raises the question: What is "salvation"? There are two sides to salvation, salvation *from* and salvation *for*. A number of things can be mentioned as things *from* which Jesus is believed to have saved humans—fear, oppression, error—but most basically and importantly, Jesus saved humans from sin and its consequences. Moreover, he saved by making it possible *for* humans to grow into maturity through faith, making it possible for them to reach their destiny in everlasting life, empowering them to form communities of justice and peace.

But precisely what did Jesus do that functions to save humanity? Clearly, overcoming sin and granting "eternal life" are things that only God can do. Both involve God's creative activity, the power of God's Spirit: only God is creator. However, as a human Jesus was savior. Even though he worked most intimately with the divine saving activity, for he was the embodiment of the divine creative Word, something that he did *humanly* brought about human salvation.

Strange as it may at first sound, Jesus was savior by his willingness to be saved, by accepting in his own living and dying the source of all overcoming of evil and all empowerment for ultimate life, God's own creative Spirit. That Spirit worked unimpeded in Jesus' ministry and flowed through his dying "obedience" to God to create the unending risen life that is the destiny of humans. As Jesus himself passed into risen life, he received that Spirit in fullness; throughout history, he shares it with those who are willing to be saved. In the profoundly theological sixth chapter of John's gospel, Jesus is asked by the crowds what they must do to obtain the unending life of which he spoke. His answer was simply "Believe in him whom God has sent" (John 6:29)— that is, in himself as risen savior.

Interestingly, and importantly, in that same passage of John's gospel, the early church immediately linked that acceptance of salvation with Christian ritual, with the celebration of the Eucharist. In obvious reference to the Eucharistic ritual and its symbolic use of bread and wine, Jesus is described as saying, "unless you eat my flesh and drink my blood," you cannot "have life in you." How is it, though, that participation in Christian rituals today is a source of salvation?

If Christian rituals—what many Christians, as we have explained, simply refer to as "the sacraments"—are celebrated as rituals, they are expressions of a community's faith: that is, its acceptance of the risen Christ and his gift of the Spirit. It is this Spirit that the community prays for and which it gratefully opens itself to receive that is the creative source of salvation. This is the Spirit of truth that works against evils that would diminish and eventually destroy people's personhood and divide them from one another. This is the Spirit that empowers them to live the new life of resurrection.

It is not only in these moments of ritual that people open themselves to the gift of God's saving Spirit. As we saw earlier, the entirety of people's lives is meant to be a process of becoming more mature as humans and as Christians. In this continuing process of initiation, however, there is a special role that rituals have: they formalize and intensify the commitment to be Christian that runs through the entirety of life. It is in a special way that in ritual actions people receive "salvation."

The Presence of the Risen Christ

This points to another aspect of Jesus' risen presence to those who believe in him, an aspect that is central to the distinctiveness of Christian rituals. These rituals are, as we mentioned, recollections of Jesus, but they actually make present what they symbolize—namely, the presence of Christ as risen. For that reason, Christian rituals, and in a special way the Eucharist, are *anamnesis* (a Greek word meaning memorial or commemoration or remembrance). They make present in symbolic action the very reality they symbolize. The Jesus who freely chose to confront death and triumphed over it in resurrection continues that choice still as, present to the assembled community, he acts as chief celebrant of the ritual. That is why, as we will see later, the Eucharistic ritual can be named a "sacrifice."

One of the great treasures of the twentieth-century development of Christian theology has been a more adequate understanding of Jesus' resurrection. For a variety of reasons, too complex for us to detail here, the original Christian awareness of Jesus' continuing presence to history after his death was, to quite an extent, lost. In Christian imagination, Jesus left the earth after his death and "went up to heaven" where he remains enthroned until he returns to earth at the end of the world. Careful study of the Christian scriptures and their witness to earliest Christian belief led in recent decades to the realization that such language and imagining about "ascending" were metaphorical descriptions of Jesus' passage into a superior way of human life and that the reality of his resurrection implied his remaining present to our history.

This, then, is what constitutes Jesus' "institution" of the Christian sacraments. He did not begin and he did not mandate the rituals themselves that emerged in the early church. But because those rituals are memorials of his life and death and resurrection, they require that he lived and died and rose. He did not establish these memorial rituals; he did that which they remember and thereby introduced a new meaning into human life.

Early Christians celebrated the ordinary events that all humans celebrate: birth, meals, marriage, initiations of all sorts, illness, reconciliation, and death. But all of these were understood now in light of their experience of Jesus as alive in their communities. The rituals they practiced remembered and made present the now risen Christ so that everyday life became the occasion to continue the work Jesus began on earth and now continues in and through the community. So strong was this belief, that the community itself was known as the "Body of Christ." It is this understanding to which we now turn.

The Christian Community as Symbol

The risen Christ through his presence to Christian communities continues to act as the chief celebrant of Christian rituals. This is possible because those communities themselves are symbols of that presence. Visible and audible in time and space, they bear witness in faith to the risen one who in resurrection is outside time and space but remains present with them. These communities can do this because they exist as "body" of the risen Christ.

To speak of the Christian communities that make up the church as "body of Christ" is more than a metaphorical way of describing the church. These communities, especially when they gather "in the name of Christ," exist and function in a way that is analogous to the existing and functioning of our human bodiliness. We humans exist symbolically because we are embodied spirits, as explained above. Though we are primarily spiritual beings, persons who think and imagine and desire and choose, we can act in this spiritual and personal way only because our bodiliness places us in time and space and allows us to communicate with one another, translating into word and gesture our inner states of consciousness.

Christians as communities of believers, visible witnesses in space and time to their belief in the presence of Christ, "situate" the risen Christ in space and time. As risen, Christians believe that he is beyond our set of dimensions and our historical happenings, but he continues as part of our history because his presence occurs in Christians' faith which is in space and time. Christ's presence, as all personal presence, is an *active* reality; it is his self-communicating with those who "hear" him. His self-gift to believers is a transforming influence in their lives that enables them to change the world in which they live and thereby cocreate with him the kingdom of God.

In this way, being symbols of the risen Christ in history, Christians not only remember Jesus but also make it possible for him to participate in the ongoing course of human history. This they do in a special way when they gather for rituals that speak their faith in who he was and what he did, but speak also their faith in what he continues to do in their midst as they ritualize that faith. However, it is good to remember that the effect of rituals is proportionate to their being genuine rituals, authentically performed by the gathered group. So, Christian communities function as body of Christ, make him present in their faith, in proportion as their rituals are active expressions of true and committed belief. This we will describe specifically and in greater detail as it is meant to occur in various sacramental rituals.

Christian Symbols as Prophetic

Christian symbols are meant in some way to reveal the presence and activity of God in human life. That implies that they are intended to "solve" a basic problem in divine/human relations. But how can any words describe what the Transcendent is all about—what symbols can function as instruments of revelation and allow God to speak to humans? Christian belief is that Jesus of Nazareth is himself the key symbol linking God and humans. The gospel of John and official church teaching has expressed this by the claim that Jesus is the divine Word embodied.

During Jesus' own public career, his disciples began implicitly and gradually to understand this by experiencing Jesus as a prophet, experiencing especially his symbolic actions. These prophetic actions, such as the multiplication of the loaves, a wonder work recorded in all four gospels, continued the tradition of Israel's prophets performing symbolic, sometimes eccentric, actions.

It is not always easy to grasp the meaning of such symbolic prophetic actions. The sixth chapter of John's gospel describes how on the day after the multiplication of the loaves, Jesus chided the crowds who had followed him around the lake because they had interpreted the action literally. Now they were expecting more miraculous free bread, and Jesus had to tell them that they had missed the point. What they should be seeking was the new bread of life, himself as living word. But the people for the most part did not understand. True, it was not easy to understand: symbols are often obscure, even ambiguous. But the deeper reason was that they did not wish to understand because this symbolic word demanded of them a response, a commitment to the revelation coming from God through the prophet Jesus. And so the crowds began at this point in Jesus' career to walk away.

Early Christianity saw this scene, the symbolism of the multiplication of the loaves, and the explanatory words of Jesus linked to the Christian Eucharist. So, in the gospel text they have Jesus saying, "Unless you eat my flesh and drink my blood, you cannot have life in you." The symbolism of bread and wine and of their transformation in Eucharist, like the symbolism of the multiplication of bread so long ago, is a prophetic word that reveals the divine offer of new life. Now as then it can be understood only in faith, and it demands the same commitment: "You must receive him whom God has sent"—Jesus as savior.

Commitment, then, is intrinsic to all the Christian sacramental rituals. Baptism is a pledge of lifelong acceptance and living out of faith in Christ and active discipleship in the church. Confirmation reiterates this pledge when one has matured somewhat in understanding and experiencing life as a Christian. The ritual of reconciliation deals with the infidelities to one's commitment that occur from time to time over the course of the years. Wedding ritualizes the commitment of two persons to one another that itself symbolizes their commitment to responsible adult life in the context of faith. The ritual of ordination expresses the specific commitment to engage in the ministry of service to the community and its life of worship. Rituals of anointing are intended to strengthen a person for perseverance in their pledge of living and dying like Christians, despite the challenge of suffering and fear of death. And throughout a Christian's life, participation in the community's celebration of Eucharist provides the opportunity to repeat one's baptismal commitment in diverse ways as the circumstances of life change.

Just as Jesus' symbolic challenge to commitment was a prophetic word, so the rituals of Christianity are "words" uttered by a prophetic community. Because they are prophetic, they speak for the community, but they also speak for God. Because they are prophetic, they accomplish what they express. They are Christians' pledge of fidelity in discipleship; they are God's pledge of unending life beyond death. These rituals are, then, a source of hope intended to sustain Christians by giving ultimate meaning to their lives and the promise that the power of God's Spirit will lead them to their destiny of union with God.

Rituals and Evil

Throughout the centuries and in practically every culture, one of the principal uses of rituals has to do with human experience of evil. People have always been threatened by the negative forces that cause suffering and harm. Such influences could be the forces of nature, like floods or earthquakes or hurricanes. Or they could be the unscrupulous behavior of humans who, moved by greed or search for power, engage in wars and destruction. Or perhaps the evil forces could be invisible, superhuman diabolic beings who work to afflict and destroy humans.

Because they did not understand how nature worked—or, for that matter, how governmental rulers worked—people in ancient times generally attributed the evil happenings in their lives to magical forces. So, they tried to meet magic with magic, trying to find rituals that unlocked the key to a particular evil force and either harnessed it or turned it away from themselves. If one studies ancient religions, one discovers that many of the sacrificial rituals that were performed had as their objective to appease some divinity that was thought to be unhappy or vengeful. People also often wore some talisman to ward off evil.

Such notions and behavior are not just something of the past. It is true that because of advances in science and medicine we better understand many of the things that threaten us and know better how to counter them. Still, many persons today are superstitious about ways to avoid evil forces and use little rituals to do so. We remember when we were growing up that wearing a medal of St. Christopher was thought to protect one from drowning. We did, though, make sure that we learned how to swim.

However, there is a deeper and more serious side to the problem of evil. What really is the source of evil? Are there such things as devils or mysterious evil forces that are capable of harming us? The number of television dramas that are based on the presence of evil in human life are a witness to widespread belief in and fear of evil. We are still wary, perhaps even worried, that there might be some evil force at work in the world. How do we ritualize today to help dispel our fears, to avoid evil, if possible?

Interestingly, one of the ways is through the theater or film. Part of ridding ourselves of undue fear of evil is to try to understand it; so, in the theater we put a face on it—something that is as old as the ancient Greek tragedies and as powerful as Shakespeare's plays. Truly artful drama gives us some insight into the deep sources of evil that lie within the human psyche, into the potential we humans have to harm ourselves and others; but it also gives an insight into the manner in which the good in humans can triumph. In his novel *East of Eden*, which obviously is intended as a retelling in modern context of the story of Adam and Eve, John Steinbeck says that ultimately there is only one plot that runs through all literature, the battle between good and evil. So, we keep telling that story, intrigued by evil even as we fear it and try to understand it.

Christian Rituals and Evil

Christianity has always had its rituals by which to confront and overcome evil. Its story is the biblical story of the unending struggle of God against chaos and sin, a story whose decisive chapter was the life and death and resurrection of Jesus of Nazareth. It ritualizes that story in the drama of the yearly liturgical cycle that commemorates and makes present the Christ mystery and brings into Christians' lives the Spirit of Christ that is the power of life overcoming sin and death. Sometimes people misunderstand the way in which the power of Christian rituals works; they may even have a semimagical view of the power of these rituals. However, at the heart of Christian ritual power over evil is something that Christianity inherited from Judaism—namely, the insight that the ultimate root of evil in human life is human abuse of freedom. This is the message of the biblical story of Adam and Eve: evil entered human history from the very beginning because of humans' choice to reject God's wisdom and follow their own destructive decisions.

The two key Christian sacramental rituals, baptism and the Eucharist (or Lord's Supper), counter this false decision to follow the path of evil by committing a person to follow the path of Christ. In baptism, before the person enters the water as a symbol of accepting the implications of Jesus' death and resurrection, he or she makes a formal rejection (through godparents, for infants) of Satan and all Satan's works and "pomps." Clearly, this ritual is not some magic formula but a basic option to avoid sin, which is the most basic form of evil. However, this option must be made again and again as one goes through life, for the temptation to evil remains. Humans can abuse one another, betray one another, be unfaithful and deceitful in dealing with one another. Repeating the ritual of the Eucharist is meant to empower Christians to resist such temptations by strengthening the commitment to good that they made in baptism.

In other words, the Christian response to evil lies in freedom. Christian rituals are meant to give persons the opportunity to join together and support one another as they work to bring justice and peace into the world. That there are evils in human life is a fact. That humans can overcome these evils is ultimately a matter of belief: belief in the power of God's Spirit, working in and through humans, to conquer evil. This is what Christians celebrate when they come together as a community of faith to ritualize.

Sacraments and Grace

Christians not only say that Jesus saves us and that Christian rituals celebrate that salvation. Many Christian communities would also say that Christian rituals "give grace." In fact, part of one traditional definition of a sacrament describes the major purpose of it as "giving grace."

As is often the case with Christian language, Christian themselves do not always know the original meaning of their own language. "Grace" is probably another instance of this. The word, like "sacrament," is a transliteration of a Latin word, in this case, *gratia*. The Latin word *gratia* originally meant either a gift or the thanks given for a gift. The word continues to be used in the latter sense in both Spanish, *gracias*, and Italian, *grazie*. So when Christians writing in Latin spoke about the "graces" (*gratias*) given to Christians by God, they meant anything that God give us for free (*gratis*). It wasn't any particular thing in itself; rather, it was anything that we received from God that we didn't deserve.

The big gift of God, or in one form of insider language, "sanctifying grace," is salvation. Nobody deserves to be saved; God loved us and God saved us, and so we get salvation for free. But we get a lot of other things for free, too: the universe, our own birth, the world we live in. These are all free gifts from God and therefore "grace." If you really think about it, most of life is "graced." If you were born into a family that is loving, that was able to send you to a good school or perhaps even to college, it wasn't because you deserve it, it was a free gift of God. If you were born in the United States rather than Haiti or Mali or Iraq, it wasn't because of any great virtue on your part. It was grace.

Not everyone is crazy about the idea of grace, of course. Some people don't think that they ever got anything for free. Whatever they got, they earned or deserved. They don't owe anybody anything. They are self-made. Of course this is a lie: at the very least, no one is their own parent; at most, it takes a tremendous amount of hubris to think you deserve sunsets, soft summer nights, and decent health. Still other people feel horribly guilty if they think that they have gotten something for free. When it comes to grace, this, too, is a mistake. The proper response to grace is thanks, not guilt. Guilt still implies that somehow people ought to deserve grace. The point of grace is that it's free, undeserved, and wonderful. Appreciation seems more in order and certainly also enjoyment. It would be insulting to God, for instance, to say, "well, OK, thanks, God, for this great day, but I'm not going to enjoy it because I don't deserve it." What ingratitude. Of course you don't deserve it; that's not the point of a gift.

When we give gifts we want people to feel happy, not surly or guilty or entitled. Writing about God's great gift of salvation, the fourteenth-century mystic Julian of Norwich wrote: "Always a cheerful giver pays only little attention to the thing he is giving, but all his desire and all his attention is to please and comfort the one to whom he is giving it. And if the receiver accepts the gift gladly and gratefully, then the courteous giver counts as nothing all his expense and labor, because of the joy and the delight that he has because he has pleased and comforted the one whom he loves."[2] Since God has given us so many wonderful free gifts (graces), the only proper thing to do is thank him and enjoy the presents. So Christians celebrate, praise God, give thanks, and really should have a wonderful time doing so.

---

2. *Julian of Norwich, Showings.* Translated by Edmund Colledge and James Walsh (New York: Paulist Press, 1978) 219.

So why aren't people more grateful? Well, if you don't really deserve all the stuff you have, than maybe, just maybe, you aren't really better than those without all the stuff. Maybe you just lucked out and they didn't. You could be just like them. Maybe you ought to help them out. Now that can be a scary thought. If you can convince yourself that you really deserve that mink-lined sink and gold-plated swimming pool, then you can also convince yourself that those who don't have such things are just lazy, good-for-nothings who could be like you, but just aren't as smart, good looking, talented, and hard working as you are. Grace undermines all such attempts to so convince ourselves and makes everyone equally special in the eyes of God. The expression, "there but for the grace of God go I" is simply the literal truth.

Love as Grace

The one thing that no one, not even the most arrogant, can refuse to recognize as grace is love. You can't buy love, you can't deserve love, you can't inherit love. You just get it. One day it happens in the lives of most people that we realize that our parents love us even though we just crashed the car, or didn't come home on time, or married that jerk our parent warned us about. Our parents loved us even though we didn't deserve it. It is a wonderful moment. Of course, sometimes it is not your parents who first show you that kind of love: it's a friend, your spouse, your child. But it happens, and it changes everything, because for some one person at least you are loved for who you are, despite all your faults. Such love is by definition undeserved and free. It is grace and, from a Christian perspective, it is divine: "God is love, and anyone who lives in love, lives in God and God in her or him" (1 John 4:6).

Psychologists tell us that unless that wonderful moment happens and we realize that some one truly loves us, we can never love. How terribly sad it must be when this happens. We cannot love until and unless we are loved. Christians, of course, believe that God loves everyone, but this love of God is actually experienced through other people: "No one has ever seen God; but as long as we love one another God will live in us and God's love will be complete in us" (1 John 4:12). As described above, Christians ought to be the tangible means by which the love of God is experienced.

The love of God that is grace, then, actually exists when the lives of people are touched. When a hungry person is fed, when a homeless person is sheltered, when a broken person is healed, when couples commit to each other in love—each of these is grace, and that is God's love at work in the world. Salvation takes place right before people's eyes. If this is grace, then, how do the "sacraments give grace"? Insofar as Christian rituals celebrate an active life of charity, they give grace. Insofar as Christian rituals strengthen the sick, pardon sinners, heal the broken, they give grace. Insofar as they celebrate and strengthen the Christian commitment to a life of maturation in selfless love, they give grace. Insofar as they celebrate and support a loving friendship and caring family life, they give grace.

Five Elements of Ritual

Given this understanding of "grace," each of the Christian rituals described below can be said to "give grace." Grace, though, always takes a particular form; it is not some undifferentiated gift, but some actual event or object or person. Christian rituals are complex, of course, and offer many different gifts, but in this book we suggest that each of the rituals includes at least five elements that aid Christians in their salvation.

First, every ritual expresses both how a community understands the world and how the ritual itself helps shape that understanding. Participating in a parade on the Fourth of July or reciting the Pledge of Allegiance does much more to inculcate patriotism in people than does reading the Declaration of Independence: tears can come to one's eyes in the first two activities, probably not in the latter. Communities keep their worldviews in existence in part by celebrating those worldviews. Young people and strangers are introduced to that worldview by participating in the rituals. In other words, rituals can tell us how we should understand the many experiences we have of the world.

The technical term for this kind of interpretation is "hermeneutic." Rituals are one form of "hermeneutic of experience"—or, if you like, one means through which a community interprets the world. A ritual can tell you what birth, adolescence, marriage, and death are all about. Christians, as we have described, have a particular way of understanding the world, and so, under-standably, their rituals celebrate and reinforce this understanding. The first element, then, contained in each of the Christian rituals discussed below is the hermeneutic of experience. Each of these rituals in its own particular way reminds Christians of how they are to interpret the world and the many ex-periences they have of it. More powerfully, these rituals gradually come to shape the way Christians see the world, and so the world as it exists for them.

Second, Christian rituals help Christians "grow up" in the sense discussed above. These rituals—again, each in its own way—challenge Christians to be-come more mature, more selfless: in short, more loving. This is the heart of Christianity, and each ritual offers the possibility of a further maturation.

Third, Christians believe that the risen Christ remains with the community. This presence, although mostly associated with Christian prayer, attends all Christian rituals. So it is in the rituals that Christians believe that they are called, nourished, and challenged by an experience of the risen Christ. Empowered by that presence, they are able to continue the work started long ago by Jesus: that is, to bring salvation to and for each other.

Fourth, the salvation we are called to bring to and for each other is embodied in service. The work that Jesus began and which the Christian community continues as the Body of Christ is to feed the hungry, to give drink to the thirsty, to welcome the stranger, to clothe the naked, and to visit the sick and imprisoned (Matt. 25:35–36). Service should be the distinguishing feature of the Christian life, and each Christian ritual should remind those celebrating of this calling.

Finally, each Christian ritual should be a celebration of friendship. The community gathers for mutual support in times of great joy or great sadness. The ritual gathering itself should tell each person attending that others share their concerns, their commitments, their hopes and their fears. Of course, Christian also gather to laugh, to cry, to eat, to drink, to dance and sing. These activities both celebrate friendship and create it. Under the best of conditions, all Christian rituals bring people together as sisters and brothers, and—again, under the best of conditions—sisters and brothers become friends.

These five elements—hermeneutic of experience, maturation, presence, service, and friendship—are shared by all Christian rituals. These are not the only means by which the rituals "give grace," but certainly they are the central means by which Christians learn to interpret their lives as Christians, grow into a selfless life, experience the presence of the risen Christ, bring that presence into existence for others through service, and come together as a community of mutual support. In short, these are important ways in which Christians experience salvation.

3

Rituals of Friendship

Human Relationships

In the process of growing toward maturity, which we have seen is
the basic pattern of humans' lives, the key experience is the development of relationships. It is by relating to a range of persons, in
many different environments, that an individual comes to know and
identify himself or herself. If such relationships are positive and
healthy, a person will enjoy a life of happiness and achievement, independent of wealth or political power or fame. If they are destructive relationships, however, the story of that person's life will likely
be a tragic one.

Some relationships seem to be common: we are all born into
families, relate to parents and siblings, and go to school as children
and relate to teachers and fellow students. Following our school
years, we choose some job or profession with which to make a living. Most of us will fall in love in early adulthood, marry, and establish a family. Then will follow years of dealing with people at work,
or recreating, or just accidentally meeting people, some of whom
will become friends, most of whom will be at best acquaintances.

Yet, there really is no common pattern we all follow. What the
course of our life experience actually is depends on the particular
people we meet in these various circumstances, on the way we deal
with them, and on the way they respond to us. The actual behavior
of parents and children to one another differs widely from family to

family. In some cases it is an enriching appreciation of one another, a spirit of support and cooperation. In other families there is a state of incessant warfare. It is with these relationships—establishing them, celebrating them, repairing them, nurturing them—that Christian rituals are concerned. But beyond such formal ritualizing of relationships within Christian communities, there is a wide range of human rituals that we use to relate to one another as humans.

Rituals of Friendship

When we relate to someone as a friend, we do such things as share meals or a drink together, we go hiking together or to a movie or just hang out. We may shake hands when we meet. A very special friend, particularly a "significant other," we kiss or hug. Such gestures symbolize the relationship we share and cherish, and repeating them confirms and deepens the bond.

Perhaps the situation of dealing with another is a business arrangement of one sort or another. We don't have any personal friendship that we need to express, but we do have to give some indication that we trust one another and intend to work together on the deal in question. So, as a sign of that trust, we seal our agreement with a handshake. Or perhaps as we leave the room after our meeting, one puts his arm around the shoulder of the other with a word of encouragement or support. In other circumstances a handshake may be the gesture used to seal reconciliation between two persons, to say that both regret the break in their relationship and to show their commitment to reestablish it.

We are accustomed to the "high five" that members of a sports team use to share their success or their commitment to working together to win. Using a "V for victory" sign lets others know that we are friendly toward them, agree with them in some action in which they are involved, share their point of view on some issue.

Of course, not all relationships are positive, and the rituals linked with them are quite different from those we have just described. Angry disagreement after a bitter argument can be made clear by slamming the door as one leaves the room. Street gangs symbolize their hostility toward one another by gestures both recognize. Picketing can be used to make it clear that the desired relationship of cooperation between management and employees has broken down. And in the tensions and conflicts that plague many families, there usually are a range of established symbols that members of the family use to show through ritual their displeasure or anger with one another.

What is important is that people learn how to relate to a variety of people, that they desire to relate honestly and openly and positively, that they develop means of cultivating ways of relating fruitfully to others—and that includes using appropriate rituals. Relating to others requires more than knowing the proper thing to do; genuine relating to others is an art. Like any art, it can be acquired only by practice. Above all, it demands that one become adept in using appropriate rituals, using them sincerely as symbols of mature relating to others.

As we go through life and encounter all the experiences we have been describing—birth, growing up, success and failure, suffering, joy, death—it is clear that these experiences involve relationships to people. We humans are not intended to live and experience as solitary individuals. Much as we prize our own distinctive individuality and freedoms, we cannot even be who we are without others to whom we are related in diverse ways. To a very large extent, the particular relationships we have had and have and how we have reacted to them determine who we are. There is nothing more meaningful in our lives than the relationships we have to others.

There are, of course, many ways in which we can relate to others: we can fear them, we can hate them, we can pity them, we can respect them, we can envy them, and we can love them. Each of these says something about the other persons, at least the way we regard them; but each also says something about ourselves. Each of them helps determine the way we experience ourselves.

Among these many possible relationships, the most precious, most cherished, and most important is love and friendship. Humans have always recognized that there is no greater gift that life can provide than a circle of friends, and especially one other who is a very close and intimate friend. This goes deeper than the comfort that comes from having someone who understands and appreciates us, someone to whom we can go for advice and consoling and support. Our own self-appreciation depends on some others thinking we are desirable as a friend, thinking that, at least for them, we are important and have some meaning.

Forming Friendships

How friendships arise and grow is, of course, a bit of a mystery. Why certain people are attracted to one another is often far from clear. Common interests, attractive personalities, shared experiences, similar family backgrounds—all these are factors, but deep friendship extends beyond these bonds. Ultimately there is no explaining friendship: thinkers have been trying to do this for centuries; one can only understand it by experiencing it.

Friendships can come into being almost instantly; there is such a thing as love at first sight. However, even in such instances friendship needs to be nurtured if it is to endure. Much as one may treasure friends and realize that there is no other possession that can match the value of genuine friendships, one must work at even the deepest of loves. One must let the other know that she or he is respected, cherished, needed, valued. Communication is the very lifeblood of intimate relationship.

Marriage Rituals

In no other relationship is all this truer than in a truly loving marriage. Even at a time when there is widespread skepticism about the possibility of lifelong fidelity and growing devotedness between two persons, there is an attractiveness in marriage that has power to lead millions to desire and risk it. Many things make up a marriage, but true friendship between the spouses is central: if it exists, the relationship can weather many a storm; if it is missing, there is a void that belies the external bonds between the two.

So, as in all friendships, over the years married lovers must learn to communicate in meaningful ways their care for each other. This they do by rituals of one sort or another, some of them like many other folks—going out to dinner together, taking vacations to places that are favorites of theirs, visiting their families across the country. Some of them treasure little rituals that are just theirs and have become familiar and special to them: morning coffee and croissants on the patio, worship together and the newspaper on Sunday, sharing their favorite piece of music. Most important, of course, are the rituals that surround and give special meaning to their lovemaking and help keep it from becoming routine.

It is not just married couples who have rituals to express and develop their relationship. All friends do. They gather to watch the World Series on television. Friday evenings are reserved for bridge games that are occasions for sharing experiences and rumors and opinions. Circles of friends come together for family events; births, graduations from college, engagements and marriages, even funerals form a series of gatherings that are marked by long-standing ritual traditions. It is these rituals, scarcely recognized as such by people, that give meaning to these events and so to people's lives, meaning they can share with one another. It is by means of these rituals that they can share their lives and themselves with one another and bond in true human community.

As we have seen in studying the meaning of the key aspects of human lived experience, each of these has been celebrated in various cultures by certain established rituals. In Christian cultures, this meaning and therefore the rituals celebrating this meaning have been transformed by the meaning coming from the life and dying and rising of Jesus of Nazareth. By these Christian rituals the meaning of what it means to be humans is transformed and "saved."

Perhaps because these sacramental aspects of human life were so all inclusive, theologians did not develop an explanation of the ritual moment of these sacraments until about the twelfth century. At that point, the term "sacrament" began to designate only the ritual element in each sacramental aspect of life, and people began to forget that "sacrament" was really something quite a bit broader. Remember, as discussed in earlier chapters, the insider word "sacrament" originally meant any symbol or ritual that God chose to mediate salvation to humans. It was just at this time that the word began to take on a more precise meaning. So theologians faced a problem: they were looking for a definition of sacrament that would fit a generic use of the term. They were unable to do this, because the various sacramental areas are analogous, they do not fit into a species: being reconciled is quite different from being recognized for ministry. The one thing that these sacramental areas had in common, however, was that each one had attached to it a special ritual: baptizing, confirming, anointing, and so on. So the rituals came to be considered the sacrament.

One of these "seven sacraments," as described by the influential twelfth-century theologian Peter the Lombard, was Christian marriage. It, though, seemed to present a particular problem. For centuries there had been no ritual ceremony, what we have come to know as a wedding, specific to Christians. Christian couples were married in the same way as any other couples in their culture; what made it a Christian marriage was that the two persons were Christian. Gradually over the centuries a Christian wedding ritual emerged, but even by the twelfth century when theologians were puzzling over the specific character of Christian marriages, an officially recognized wedding ritual was not considered necessary—common law marriages were also recognized as true marriages. It was not until the Council of Trent in the sixteenth century that there was a determined ritual required for a valid marriage. Since that time people's common understanding is that the wedding ceremony is the sacrament of marriage.

Marriage, Sacrament of the Relationship to God

Theological reflection makes it clear, however, that, important as is the wedding ritual might be, the sacrament of marriage is the two persons in their relation to one another. Christian marriage—as a matter of fact, any marriage—is a process in which two persons are meant to be increasingly bonded to one another. Although sexual bonding and the limitation of sexual activity of the spouses to one another have always been seen as central to the lifelong commitment of marriage, this itself is grounded in something deeper: the commitment to a lasting and distinctive love and friendship. So, theologians decided that what made a marriage valid for Christians was not the wedding or sexual relations but the commitment of the two people to each other. This means that the two ministers of a Christian marriage are actually the couple. The presiding minister or priest is just a witness to the commitment being made.

This was a big change in the history of marriage. Historically, the friendship dimension of marriage had not always and in every culture been stressed. In some contexts marriage was considered essentially a social arrangement for continuing the family name, preserving family property, or cementing diplomatic arrangements. In more recent centuries there has been greater attention paid to the romantic love aspect and resultant greater appreciation of the sacramentality of friendship in general, but this is due to the understanding of marriage as a commitment between two people that originated in the twelfth century.

If friendship is considered at the heart of a Christian marriage, the wedding ritual takes on a significance specifically linked with the Christ meaning. Whereas in earlier times the marriage ceremony was viewed more legalistically as a contract, and this view was incorporated into church law that defined a valid marriage as a contract, the designation now used is "covenant." This may not seem to be a major change, but it picks up the biblical connotations of "covenant" and the theology of the Pauline writings.

The Hebrew Bible's approach to human marriage was deeply influenced by the prophet Hosea, who used marriage as a metaphor for the relation between Yahweh and Israel. While this obviously was intended to carry over into divine-human relationships in the personal relation of loving spouses, the carryover of meaning went the opposite direction also: Yahweh's relation to the chosen people threw light on the relationship of people in marriage. The fidelity of God became a model for the fidelity expected in marriage, but so also did God's unconditional love. As a result of this prophetic insight, the institution of marriage in Judaism at the time of Jesus was markedly more personal than it was in most surrounding populations.

In the theology of the Pauline epistles the link between Christian marriage and the mystery of Jesus' act of salvation is more than metaphorical. Especially in the Epistle to the Ephesians, the relation between husband and wife is compared to Jesus' dying self-gift to believers. The relationship between Christian spouses is sacramental, revelatory, of the continuing self-gift of the risen Christ to his followers. A Christian marriage is meant to be a symbol of the presence of God in Christ created by the shared faith and love of the two persons as they relate to one another in all the diverse aspects of their life together.

Anyone who has been married or been a child (and that covers most of us) realizes that self-giving is essential if any relationship is going to work. The changes true friendship entails can be minor (that crazy toilet seat thing) or major (serious illness, financial problems, the rest of her or his family). Just dealing with these issue changes each of the people involved. The addition of children further complicates matters. Now there are at least three people who must adapt to each other's quirks. What makes all of this possible, from a Christian perspective, is the spirit of the risen Christ who empowers all concerned to become more loving in the process of sometimes drastic and wrenching changes.

The examples are endless. There are parents who work overtime to put their kids through college and in so doing give up any "life" of their own. Even more dramatically, there are parents who risk imprisonment and even death to sneak across the border to the United States in order to provide a future for their children. There are children who take care of their elderly parents as great cost, both financially and emotionally. There are spouses who care for their mates through mental illness, emotional collapse, serious physical illness, financial disaster, and disease and death. On a daily basis, and in a thousand little ways, friendship, and particularly marriage, embodies (sacramentalizes) the central Christian purpose of Christ's death and resurrection: "No one has greater love than this, to lay down one's life for one's friends" (John 16:12).

This is not to suggest that love is always simply passive. There are times when to be loving means not to agree, not to go along, not to accept what the partner is doing. The hardest love of all is that which must say "no" if it is to be true love. If one really wants the best for the other, there are those awful times when the most loving thing to say is "no more; I must leave you if you cannot change. I love you too much to support your self-destruction." These are the crucifixions that parents, children, spouses (in short, friends) bear for each other in the hope that a resurrection can still occur. And, sadly of course, it doesn't always work.

Importantly and from a Christian perspective, this self-giving, with all the suffering and pain that can entail, does lead to the resurrection. In the process of self-giving, even when that giving is not or cannot be reciprocated, the person has the possibility of growing into a more loving, more fulfilled, more joyful, and even more divine person—or at least Christians so believe. For to act out of real love is to act like the God that was revealed in Jesus. For most people, salvation takes place in the everyday acts of going to work, making the kids' lunches, fixing up the house, saving for college, nursing a sick parent or spouse—and, of course, in those special meals, in that unexpected present, the long-awaited vacation, the graduation where the child becomes an adult in front of your very eyes. Finally, there are the quiet moments, where holding hands becomes all there is in the universe and to speak would be unnecessary; only a smile and slight squeeze of the hands will do.

The Wedding Ritual

As we saw of marriages in general, such a sharing demands expressions of various kinds—that is, rituals that can help the relationship grow and mature. While it is not by itself sufficient, the wedding ritual plays a very special and determining part here. It places the sacramental relationship in the public sphere where it gives witness to the hope of personal devotedness and lasting fidelity. Moreover, as a ritual in which the entire community participates, a wedding provides a pledge of support during the years ahead. Finally, since stable married life is an element needed in a culture, the wedding ritual helps to guarantee the seriousness and genuineness of the relationship between the two persons.

In the case of a Christian wedding ceremony, the community that is assembled to witness and join in the celebration of the committed love of the couple is a community of faith. For them the profession of lifelong commitment can and should be seen as a symbol of the saving love of Christ who is present to the community. Besides, the married couple is in the ritual a reflection and exemplification of the kind of bond that links the risen Christ to his followers. In a distinctive way the wedding ritual is an important part of the church's ministry of evangelization.

As just mentioned, in the wedding ceremony the agents of the action are the two people being married. They are the ministers of the sacrament. Someone else does not marry them; they marry one another. This has been widely overlooked on the popular level where people still think of the officiating priest or pastor as being the minister of the sacrament. They generally say, "Father or Pastor so-and-so married us." In reality, the ordained minister acts not as the agent of the ritual but as a required witness, officially representing the broader Christian church. However, he or she is not the only required witness; most churches also demand that there be two others, the best man and brides-maid, who represent the community and can from that point onward attest to the solemn promise made by the married couple. There is nothing intrinsic to the character of the marriage ritual that these requirements be met, but they have been established because while the wedding is intensely personal it is not private. Marriages exist for the sake of the two persons and then for the sake of their children, but also for the sake of society. It is important for society to know who is married to whom.

Because marriage and establishment of families is so basic an element in human societies, every culture has distinctive rituals in which the couple ex-presses their pledge of lasting fidelity to one another, rituals in which some representatives at least of their "neighbors" witness to the new relationship. As we saw, it is the two individuals being married who are the essential agents in the ritual—in Christian terms the "ministers of the sacrament"—but the wedding (or its equivalent) is not a purely private affair but an action that places the spouses in a new role and status in their society.

Consequently, there have been and are a wide range of wedding rituals that are celebrated in various cultural contexts. In Christian circles there is a general similarity in the weddings that take place in various denominations: usually in a church building decorated specially for the occasion, the couple are accompanied by their families and friends, and there is an official eccle-siastical representative (a priest or minister) before whom the bride and groom make their solemn pledges of self-gift to one another. Not that it is a part of the wedding ritual as such, but the church service is usually followed by a reception at which family and friends eat, drink, dance, and make appropriate speeches and toasts to congratulate the newlyweds.

In our society, of course, many couples are married in a civil ceremony. Before a civil magistrate, often in a public office building of some sort, perhaps with a few family or friends as witnesses, the two persons pronounce their pledges to one another. It is more common, too, that the place in which the wedding is celebrated—even when it is an official church wedding—is neither in a church nor in a civic building but in a home, garden, or other special outdoor setting.

In many other religions or cultures—including Judaism, Hinduism, and

Islam—there are established wedding rituals that create and celebrate publicly the new bond between the married couple. Many of these are elaborate and traditional, and most involve a gathering of family and friends. Despite the wide range of such rituals, and the fact that in some societies the marriage is an arrangement between two families, there is a recognition that the heart of the wedding ritual itself is the pledge of bride and bridegroom to one another.

Five Elements of Ritual

Religious weddings, then, no matter how diverse, exemplify in striking fashion the five aspects of ritual we have noted.

Hermeneutic of Experience

Weddings function in a special way to provide a hermeneutic of experience. The new relationship between bride and bridegroom will provide a context and point of view for interpreting the events that occur to them throughout their life together. Ideally, it will provide a dimension in their experience that will throw light on everything else. As one commentator on the change that occurred for him because of his married relationship observed: "Before I met my wife and married her, everything was in black and white; after I fell in love with her and married, everything was in technicolor."

Of course, the self-giving symbolized in the wedding ceremony may not be apparent even to the couple during the wedding itself. All too often weddings become more a symbol of the wealth of the families involved. Selfishness all too often has more do with the preparation for the ceremony than any idea of selflessness. Still the words of vows can always drift back to the spouses in moments of crisis: "Ah, so this is the 'worse' part of 'for better or for worse.' Now I see what I was getting into!" One may even smile at the naiveté of the wedding and fondly and lovingly reshape what that day actually meant. The wedding itself may well change over time as it interprets and is reinterpreted by the actual life of the spouses together.

Presence

If, as we saw, personal presence in its fullest form is a question of a person being for another, then wedding rituals that are essentially two persons committing themselves to be uniquely for one another are expressive of and creative of presence. So also, on the occasion of a wedding, are family and friends present to and for the newlyweds in sharing their joy and promising support. And when the wedding takes place in a religious setting—when it is celebrated during a Christian Eucharist—there is a sense of divine approval and support along with an implicit awareness that the ritual of human love reflects the greater mystery of divine care and concern.

Maturation

A wedding opens up for the two people a new opportunity to mature as human beings. If loving is at the very heart of one growing in maturity—and it is—then loving and being loved in the intimacy of marriage provides an unparalleled situation for personal maturation. The wedding ritual can and should be a key symbolic moment in the process of growing up into genuine adulthood. Obviously, as stated above, the actual attainment of maturity by the two persons will depend on the way in which the promise of the wedding day is translated into the everyday happenings of their life together. Still, the symbolic power of that ritual will remain as a challenge and resource.

Service

Few, if any, occasions of human interaction are deeper statements of one person's pledge to be of service to another. While the formulations of marriage vows vary from one wedding to another, they all express something like the familiar promise "in sickness and in health, for better or for worse, till death do us part." Moreover, the kind of service that is foreseen (or probably more often, not foreseen) is not that of reluctant obligation but of loving care and concern for another.

Friendship

Finally, it needs no further explanation of the statement that friendship is central to the wedding ritual. While other friendships can complement and enrich the relationship between the married couple, their relationship to one another can and should continue to enjoy a central place in their lives. Probably the family and friends gathered for the wedding have no wish for the newlyweds more heartfelt than that the life upon which they are embarking will be a growing and enduring friendship.

Dissolution of Marriage

So far marriage has been described in its ideal state. Marriage should be a public witness to the self-sacrifice that transforms people. Marriage should help people become more loving, more giving, and, because of this, more fulfilled. It is the usual way people are saved. As such, marriage is the most powerful symbol (sacrament) of how God loves us.

However, marriage does not always work out that way. Marriages can also be unhealthy relationships, destructive for all those involved. Marriages can be based on selfishness from the start: on exploitation, dominance, fear, or desperation. Such marriages may change over time and evolve into a loving relationship despite their rocky starts, but often they do not.

Even when marriages do start out with noblest of intentions, illness or poverty can overwhelm and gradually wear down the high ideals celebrated in the wedding ceremony. The couples may find that they are, in the end, simply incompatible, or changes in the lives of one or both of the spouses may be too much for the relationship to handle. For any and all these reasons, marriages fail. Recent estimates suggest that 40 percent of marriages in the United States end in divorce.

Failed marriages can be and often are terrible experiences. Children can feel guilty or betrayed. Spouses not only feel those same feelings but are also often left alone to face increased financial burdens. In the United States, these burdens and the obligation to raise the children fall disproportionately on women.

Christianity has wrestled with the problem of failed marriages almost from its inception. Certainly, the ideal of marriage has always been a lifelong and irreversible commitment. Jesus states this clearly in Mark 10:11–12. When asked on what grounds a husband might divorce his wife, Jesus replied, "Therefore what God has joined together, let no one separate." Many Christians down to the present day have understood this to mean that dissolution of marriage is forbidden to Christians under any circumstances. If a couple must separate, they are nonetheless still married and they are not free to marry again.

Within the scriptures themselves, however, there seem to be exceptions to this strict interpretation of Jesus' words. When Matthew (5:32; 19:9) reported this teaching of Jesus, he offered a slightly different version: "Whoever divorces his wife, except for *porneia*, causes her to commit adultery and whoever marries a divorced woman commits adultery." The meaning of this Greek word, *porneia*, has been and still is much discussed by Christians. Some suggest that it means adultery, so that if one party in a marriage commits adultery, the marriage is thereby dissolved and the innocent party is free to marry again. Most recent scholars suggest that the word refers to the Jewish laws of consanguinity and so allow for the dissolution of marriage on those grounds.

In his first letter to the Corinthians, Paul repeats the teaching of Jesus that a wife should not separate from her husband (1 Cor. 7:10–11). In addition, he gives his own advice concerning the situation where one spouse becomes Christian and other remains unconverted: if the pagan spouse refuses to live with the Christian spouse, then the marriage can be dissolved. This has been known as the Pauline privilege in Christian tradition and offers another early exception to the stricter teaching contained in Mark.

By the fourth century, the Council of Nicea offered further advice on what to do if a marriage failed. The council accepted those back into the church who had abandoned their first spouses and remarried, but only if they had repented for their sins. After suitable penance, their second marriage would be allowed and they could return to the Christian community. Again, while the seriousness of a lifelong commitment was upheld, exceptions were allowed for cases where the ideal had not been achieved.

The Eastern Orthodox churches, based on teachings like that of Nicea, have long held that marriage could "die." When a marriage is no longer viable, when it becomes destructive for all the parties involved and there is no hope of reviving the relationship, then the couple may separate. An innocent or repentant spouse may then remarry, but the second marriage is celebrated with both joy and sorrow, in a spirit of repentance and compassion. "Compassion" is the operative word here. Although the ideal remains that of indissoluble marriage, the Orthodox churches recognize that compassion must be extended to those who fail, despite their best efforts, to live up to the ideal of lifelong friendship and union.

The Roman Catholic Church offers fewer possibilities for the dissolution of a marriage. The Pauline privilege can be applied as well as a "Petrine" privilege. The latter case applies when a Christian marries a non-Christian; such a marriage can be dissolved, but only by the pope. Since both of these instances require special papal permission, they are quite rare. A marriage may also be dissolved by ecclesiastical consent if the marriage was never physically consummated. Otherwise Roman Catholics do not recognize dissolution of a marriage for any reason and will not allow communion to those who remarry after a divorce. This has been a serious problem within that community, causing many divorced and remarried Catholics to simply leave the church.

Roman Catholics do allow for "annulments," however. That is, a church court or official can rule that a sacramental marriage never happened. If, for instance, it can be shown that a true commitment was never made, or that such a commitment was not possible for one of the spouses, than an annulment is granted. The annulment simply states that marriage never happened. Both spouses are then free to marry for what technically would be the first time. The difficulty of obtaining an annulment can differ from place to place and from time to time and again can make for some awkward situations, especially if a marriage is annulled after many years and only one of the partners wishes the annulment.

Other Christian groups vary in their teaching on marriage. Some do not allow for dissolution of marriage for any reason, nor do they allow for remarriage. Others allow for dissolution, but the spouses are not free to marry again. Still others allow dissolution and remarriage for specific reasons, such as adultery, based on the teaching in Matthew. Based on the teaching that all are sinners, some Christian groups allow for dissolution and remarriage for any reason that the spouses feel before God is sufficient. In all cases, however, the dissolution of a marriage is understood as a great sadness, even when it is clear that it is by far the best thing for all concerned.

Christians live in an imperfect world and down through the centuries, they have wrestled with the question of how to reconcile the ideal of indissoluble marriage with the realities of human frailty and, sometimes, just the sheer overwhelming burdens of life. One can only surmise that that wrestling will continue for many more centuries.

4

Rituals of Christian Initiation

Earlier we spoke about the fact that there is a continuous sequence of experiences by which each of us grows from infancy to adulthood and develops her or his personhood and self-identity. For one who is a Christian, this process is meant to be deepened and absorbed into the process of becoming a Christian. Just as one is meant to be initiated into life by being initiated into a community of fellow humans, so a Christian is meant to be initiated into the community of faith, the church, and so become increasingly Christian. The whole of a Christian's life should be a growing initiation into Christianity, into living the mystery of Christ with others. This should imply that at each stage of life a Christian finds and lives out the additional meaning that comes to human life because of the meaning of Jesus' life and dying and rising, and that one does this by participating in a Christian community with deepening understanding and commitment. However, every life has a beginning from which it grows, and so, too, the Christian life. Christian life begins, not surprisingly, with a ceremony: a celebration of a new kind of life. Perhaps this is why another name for baptism is "christening." Baptism is the initiation of the life-long process of becoming a Christian.

Early Christian Initiation

From the very beginning of Christianity there was a realization that a person needed to be initiated into the Christian community. The initiation ceremony, also from the very beginning, consisted of a blessing that accompanied an immersion in water or at least a symbolic washing in water—that is, a baptism. Baptism had been practiced in Judaism for a long time before the time of Jesus as a ritual that cleansed one from impurity. Jesus himself was baptized by John "the Baptist" in the River Jordan. Therefore, the early followers of Jesus were just following a fairly common Jewish practice when they initiated new members into their community with a baptism. It was taken for granted that this is what Jesus wished to be the initiation ceremony for the group. According to the gospel of Matthew, Jesus commissioned his followers with the charge to "Go, therefore and make disciples of all nations, baptizing them in the name of the Father and of the Son and of the Holy Spirit" (Matt. 28:19).

In his letters, Paul also assumes that the followers of Jesus had been baptized, and he goes on to explain that this baptism united them with Jesus' death and resurrection: "Therefore we have been buried with him by baptism into death, so that, just as Christ was raised from the dead by the glory of the Father, so we too might walk in the newness of life" (Rom. 6:4). According to Paul, those baptized descend into the dark side of water—death and chaos, powerlessness and fear—and come back to life from water: new birth growing out of life-giving water. Here Paul is drawing on a very powerful and ancient symbolism. Water was, and is, both life and death for humans. Too much water in the form of powerful ocean tides or raging floods can drown us with its awesome power. Too little water leeches us of strength, and we quickly die of thirst. Of course, this is true not only of humans. Every farmer dreads both flood and drought. Too much water at the wrong time can mean crops die and famine can result. Too little water, and crops never grow and again famine can result. Water is death for all creation; water is life for all creation. It should come as no surprise that the probes sent to Mars are looking for evidence of water, since evidence of water would be evidence for the possibility of life. Most societies celebrate in some way the life-and-death-dealing power of water. Christians inherited the symbolism of water directly from Judaism.

According to Paul, baptism makes people into something new in the Spirit of the risen Christ. Old social conventions no longer apply: "For by the one Spirit we were all baptized into one body—Jew or Greeks, slaves or free—and we were all made to drink of one Spirit" (1 Cor. 12:13). Christians are meant to be a new creation, alive in the Spirit, reborn from the water of baptism. The close association of the rebirth of baptism, the new life of the Spirit, and the living out of a new kind of existence comes together graphically in the second chapter of the Acts of the Apostles. The Spirit of God descends dramatically on the followers of Jesus like a violent wind and tongues of fire. Filled with the Spirit, Peter gave a rousing sermon heard miraculously in several languages. The passage concludes:

> So those who welcomed his message were baptized, and that day about three thousand persons were added. They devoted themselves to the apostles' teaching and fellowship, to the breaking of the bread and the prayers. Awe came upon everyone, because many wonders and signs were being done by the apostles. All who believed were together and had all things in common; they would sell their possessions and goods and distribute the proceeds to all, as any had need. Day by day, as they spent much time together in the temple, they broke bread at home and ate their food with glad and generous hearts, praising God and having the goodwill of all the people. And day by day the Lord added to their number those who were being saved. (Acts 2:41–47)

The earliest Christian records understand the initial ceremony of baptism as united with the Spirit-filled life that marks Christians as different. They were empowered to live the life of selfless love that Jesus had lived and which is now possible in the Spirit of the risen Christ. Not surprisingly, baptism was also closely linked to the celebration of the life and death of Jesus, the communal meal and prayer called by the author of the Acts of the Apostles "the breaking of the bread." Later Christians will call "the breaking of the bread" by many other names: "Sunday Service," "Holy Communion," "Eucharist," and "the Lord's Supper." (In this book we use these terms interchangeably but most commonly use "Eucharist" to refer to this ritual.) The link between the Spirit that filled Christians and empowered them to live the selfless love to which they were called, the baptism that initiated that life, and the weekly celebration that renewed that first commitment—all of these were understood to be a unity from earliest times.

A Little More Background

At first, converts to Christianity were adults. Jews or Gentiles who heard the preaching about Jesus, became interested, learned about this new way of life, and eventually signed up. The ceremonies for this initiation were fairly simple.

The account as we have it from Justin Martyr writing in the second century in Rome is pretty straightforward:

> I will also relate the manner in which we dedicated ourselves to God when we had been made new through Christ; lest, if we omit this, we seem to be unfair in the explanation we are making. As many as are persuaded and believe that what we teach and say is true, and undertake to be able to live accordingly, are instructed to pray and to entreat God with fasting, for the remission of their sins that are past, we are praying and fasting with them. Then they are brought by us where there is water, and are regenerated in the same manner in which we were ourselves regenerated. For, in the name of God, the Father and Lord of the universe, and of our Saviour Jesus Christ, and of the Holy Spirit, they then receive the washing with water. (*First Apology*, chapter 61)[1]

A little later he adds:

> But we, after we have thus washed him who has been convinced and has assented to our teaching, bring him to the place where those who are called brethren are assembled, in order that we may offer hearty prayers in common for ourselves and for the baptized (illuminated) person, and for all others in every place, that we may be counted worthy, now that we have learned the truth, by our works also to be found good citizens and keepers of the commandments, so that we may be saved with an everlasting salvation. Having ended the prayers, we salute one another with a kiss. There is then brought to the president of the brethren bread and a cup of wine mixed with water; and he taking them, gives praise and glory to the Father of the universe, through the name of the Son and of the Holy Ghost, and offers thanks at considerable length for our being counted worthy to receive these things at His hands. And when he has concluded the prayers and thanksgivings, all the people present express their assent by saying Amen. This word Amen answers in the Hebrew language to (the Greek) *genoito* (so be it). And when

---

1. Justin was converted to Christianity around the year 130 C.E. He taught Christianity as a philosophy first in Ephesus and then in Rome. He wrote two apologies for Christianity as well as a dialogue with the Jew, Trypho. He was martyred in Rome ca. 165 C.E. An account of his martyrdom based on official court reports still survives. The passages from Justin's *First Apology* that appear here were taken from the translation of that work found online at http://www.newadvent.org/fathers/0126.htm. The Web site is a convenient source for translations of the writings of many early Christian writers.

the president has given thanks, and all the people have expressed
their assent, those who are called by us deacons give to each of
those present to partake of the bread and wine mixed with water over-
which the thanksgiving was pronounced, and to those who are absent they carry away a portion. (*First Apology*, chapter 65)

Justin mentions no particular minister for baptism, and the link between baptism and the Lord's Supper is immediate. Justin presumes that those to be
initiated have been properly trained and that they realize what they are getting
into. Later, the process of becoming a Christian would become more formalized.

By the fourth century, several changes had taken place in this fairly simple
ceremony. The usual minister was now the *episcopos* (bishop) or the delegate
of the *episcopos*, the *presbyteros* (later presbyter or priest). (A description of these
different ministries in early Christianity is provided in chapter seven in this
volume.) The ceremony usually was celebrated at Easter Sunday Vigil after a
forty-day period of training and fasting, later known as "Lent." Those enrolled
in the process of training to become Christians were known as "catechumens"
(literally, "those to be instructed"). People could remain catechumens for decades before deciding to actually finish their training and get baptized. The
great bishop Augustine of Hippo was enrolled as a catechumen by his parents
when he was a child but didn't get baptized until he was in his thirties. Later,
we take a look at the reasons for this odd practice, but for now it is enough to
know that one started the process of becoming a Christian by becoming a
catechumen.

Once the period of instruction ended, those who wished to be baptized
had to come to the church and announce their intention to be baptized. They
were accompanied by Christians who would vouch for them and assist them
in their training both before and after baptism. These sponsors would be
known in later centuries as "godparents" or "sponsors," the spiritual parents
of this new creature in the Spirit. Exorcism would take place to remove the
demons that were understood to inhabit the non-Christian world. Finally,
the big day would come, usually, as we have mentioned, at the Easter Vigil.
The water for the baptism was blessed and exorcised, the Spirit was called
down upon those assembled, and a sign of the cross was made over the water.
Each person was immersed in water three times in the name of the Father, the
Son, and the Spirit. The heads of those just baptized were anointed with oil,
their feet were washed, and they were clothed in a new white garment that
they wore during all of Easter week. Finally, hands were laid on the newly
baptized by the bishop. Through this ritual action, they received "the gift of

the Spirit." Some places followed this ritual by giving the new Christians lighted candles or lamps. All then participated in the Eucharist for the first time.

Some variations, of course, existed. In the Syrian churches, for example, the entire bodies of the catechumens were anointed with oil by the deacon or deaconess before baptism. This anointing was understood to bestow "the gift of the Spirit" before the actual baptism. Therefore, no laying on of hands occurred after the baptism. Some places gave the newly baptized members milk and honey after the ceremony to symbolize their spiritual entry into the "land of milk and honey," a name given in scripture for Israel, itself a symbol for Christians of their own community.

Then as now, the meaning of the initiation ritual was quite clear: a person was beginning a new life; the initiation was compared to being born again. One assumed a new identity. One was now a Christian, and this was meant to change the meaning of everything thereafter in the person's life. All her or his actions were to be part of the Christian community's mission to help bring about the reign of God. The process of maturing was deepened now as the baptized person over the years increasingly took on the values, accepted the responsibilities, and lived out the concern for others that characterized Christian discipleship. Christian initiation was more than the original ritual of the baptismal ceremony; instead, it was a lifelong process of growth, a deepening relation to the risen Christ expressed through a deepening relationship to one's fellow humans.

Infant Baptism

At the very beginning, of course, and for about four centuries, the baptizing ritual was chiefly an action that initiated adults into the church, though whole families were also admitted together. Baptism was a public profession of a basic choice: the choice to follow the risen Christ and share in his continuing mission in history. However, once Christianity became the official religion of the Roman Empire, which meant that most people were baptized, baptism became increasingly a ritual performed for infants.

Christians disagree about the baptism of infants, but from roughly the fourth through the sixteenth century this was the common practice and remains so today among the majority of Christians. Generally, the ritual for the baptizing of infants follows that for adults. The commitment to become a Christian and the examination of the fitness for so doing fell now, however, not on the baby, but on the godparents. Their role became very important, for they were standing in for the infant in pledging their commitment to Christianity. They now had the obligation to see that the child was raised as a Christian. The community, in the person of the godparents, took on the role of nurturing the child in the faith.

As noted above, however, some Christians in the fourth and fifth centuries put off baptism for their children and themselves until they could make their own commitment. They did this for two reasons—one admirable, and the other not so admirable. First, they wished to wait until they were really personally committed to living the Christian life, not an easy thing to do in the cruel world of the late Roman Empire. Second, some wanted to be able to live a non-Christian life for as long as possible before committing to Christianity. They wanted a successful career, sexual affairs, and political power first. Then in their old age, or perhaps on their deathbed, they could become Christians and give up sin. The emperor Constantine, for example, was only baptized when dying. In fact, he kept a bishop at his side at all times, just in case. He wanted to die a Christian but felt that to keep his position, he needed to commit very un-Christian acts, including murdering a number of his own family.

At the very least, one can see in this odd practice that people felt that Christianity should entail a real commitment. You shouldn't get baptized until you were ready to really "walk the talk." Christianity was supposed to make a difference in the way one lived. Until you were ready to really live that way, it was much more honest not to get baptized at all.

Reasons for Infant Baptism

What about infants, then? They couldn't make a commitment for themselves, and by the time they were old enough to do so, they were already baptized. Why would Christians baptize infants if they couldn't make the commitment necessary for living out a Christian life?

There are at least two reasons that many Christians feel infants should be baptized. The first is probably the more ancient reason and also least likely to convince a modern reader. At least from the second century on, Christians worried about what would happen if someone died who had not been baptized. According to the Gospel of John, Jesus had said, "No one can enter God's kingdom without being born of water and Spirit" (John 3:5). Did that mean everyone not baptized would go to hell? That didn't seem fair. So as early as the second century, Christians began to speculate that anyone who wanted to be baptized and just didn't get to it for some reason could be saved. Maybe even those who truly desired to do God's will but never heard about Jesus were "really" baptized by that desire. This was called "baptism by desire" and was understood by those who accepted it as just as good as baptism by water.

Then there were those cases of jailors or even soldiers or judges who were so impressed by the Christians that they joined them in martyrdom without any chance of being baptized. These brave souls were considered to be baptized "by blood." Baptism by blood or by desire could cover almost anyone of good will, and some Christians down through the centuries have argued that the "real" church, the "real" community of the saved, is made up of all just people, Christian or not, baptized or not. The actual ritual of baptism in this understanding is not absolutely necessary for salvation. Of course, not all Christians believed this, then or now, but historically this openness has been far more frequent than even most Christians are aware.

Still some Christians worried. What about infants? Do *they* need to be baptized to be saved? They can't even really "desire" to be baptized, so that answer won't help. As early as the third century, Christian writers were recommending that children be baptized as early as possible to make sure they would participate in the life of the risen Christ. That way, even if they died before they could make the personal commitment necessary for adult baptism, they would be saved. As infant baptism became more common, the custom grew to baptize infants as soon after birth as possible to make sure they didn't slip into hell through neglect.

It seemed so mean, though, to think that God would send innocent babies to hell. They couldn't even really sin since they could not make the necessary judgment to do so. Speculation was ventured about a special place for infants who died without baptism. A place not quite heaven, but definitely not hell, called "limbo" (literally, "the border") was postulated. Maybe babies who died without baptism went there. No one really knew, but most parents didn't want to take that chance. More interestingly, among Western Christians, the ceremony of baptism started to be extended, ending only when the baptized Christian was old enough to make their own commitment. We will speak more about this in a moment.

The first reason, then, why Christians baptize infants was (and is) because they are afraid that infants might not be saved if they aren't baptized. As described above, Christian ritual celebrates liberation from evil; in insider language, sin is forgiven, and we are reconciled with God. Down through Christian history, some Christians have argued that everyone, even infants, is involved in sin and evil. Therefore, they do deserve to go to hell unless they are chosen by God to be saved, and the sign of that salvation is baptism. Therefore, infants must be baptized as soon as possible after birth. This particular approach, although rightly acknowledging that the world we are born into is already evil and that salvation comes from God alone, can also be understood in a sense that sees baptism as a kind of magic.

In the worst of cases, parents who haven't seen the inside of a church since their wedding suddenly get scared that their babies need baptism. Some close relatives or friends who are equally unfamiliar with the interior of a church are chosen as godparents. A wonderful party is planned. The baby is baptized, and then anything to do with the church is promptly forgotten until it is time to marry the grown child. The scramble to find a suitable church begins again. Clearly, this is not what baptism was meant to be. In fact, many, maybe most, churches refuse to baptize such children. The community insists that both the parents and godparents must be part of the community the child is about to join, or at least they must intend to join that community and demonstrate this commitment by taking the necessary training in Christianity. If the child is going to be initiated into a Christian community, then a real commitment must exist on the part of the parents and godparents to be part of the community and raise the child as a member of the community. Otherwise, it's just social custom or, worse, magic pure and simple.

At the beginning of this section, we wrote that the whole of a Christian's life should be a growing initiation into Christianity. Baptism may be a beginning, but it is only a beginning. Each day, each year, Christians should grow into their baptisms, allowing the Spirit of the risen Christ to enlighten and strengthen them to live the kind of life that Jesus lived. It is in light of the ongoing nature of baptism that infant baptism can make sense, and this is the second reason Christians feel infants should be baptized. The community, and more particularly the family of the baptized infant, is committing itself to training this young life in the ways of being Christian. From his or her earliest days, the youngster is surrounded by those who teach him or her how to see the world as Christians see it and how to live in the world as Christians do. Parents, godparents, and the larger community ought to model Christianity in their lives so that the child baptized into that family and community breathes in the Christianity all around them. Just like the adults around them, they will have many chances, and probably one particular celebration, in which they make this world their own.

For those Christians who practice infant baptism, this makes perfect sense. Why not raise your child to be a Christian if that is what you firmly believe? Wouldn't it be weird not to? It would be like raising a child without any morals or manners or civic pride because you wanted to let them decide if such customs are worthwhile once they are adults. This is strangely to assume that not teaching children anything is not also a way of teaching them. It teaches them that everything is relative and it doesn't really matter what anyone does or believes. Life is like laundry detergent: all the brands are basically the same; any one you pick is just fine.

Christians, and actually most people, don't believe any way of life is "just fine." Some ways of life are cruel, mean, and destructive for everything and everyone they touch. Some ways of life make for great unhappiness and misery. Most parents don't want their children to be cruel, miserable, and unhappy. So they teach them ways to be kind, joyful, and happy. Christians believe that living like a Christian will effect this kind of life, so they teach it to their children. If baptism is really the beginning of a Christian life, then surely, they would argue, it should start right from the beginning. This gives children a chance to grow into the life that their parents think will make them most happy.

Confirmation: Baptismal Initiation Continued

During the first few centuries, as we have described, the baptizing of the new Christians was followed by an anointing with special oil called "chrism." This was done by the bishop who in the early centuries ordinarily officiated at the initiation ritual. The bishop would also give "the gift of the Spirit" by laying his hands on the newly baptized person. After a few centuries, this anointing was detached from the baptism ritual but remained reserved to the bishop and therefore took place as a distinct ritual that became known as "confirmation." This separation of baptizing and anointing did not take place in Eastern Christianity but only in the West where it has remained the practice up to the present in many Christian communities.

By the twelfth century, confirmation was understood as a separate ceremony from baptism, but in its origins, it is really just that last part of the ancient baptism ceremony. It got separated from the other parts of the ceremony originally because the bishop couldn't be present at all baptisms of infants and, for the reasons given above, parents and pastors didn't want to put off the baptism until the bishop showed up. He might not show up in your little village for years or even decades. So confirmation slowly became a kind of "coming of age" ceremony. Children who had reached roughly the age of puberty were brought before the bishop who questioned them on the Christian life, then anointed them with oil and laid his hands on their heads. They were thus understood to receive the Spirit and the strength to lead a Christian life.

This division was unfortunate, perhaps, since it separated two important parts of the initiation ceremony—the baptism itself and the anointing and laying on of hands that symbolized the coming of the Spirit. Still, it did allow those already baptized to make their own commitment to the Christian life as young adults.

Why Baptism Only Once

One might wonder why Christians in former centuries didn't just do what might seem obvious to pragmatic, modern folk like us. Why not just let people undergo baptism again when they were old enough to make up their own minds? Have one baptism for infants to make the parents happy, and then if and when they wanted to, people could do another baptism to show their personal commitment. Curiously enough, from the second century on, there has been a very strong reluctance on the part of almost all Christian groups to perform baptism more than once in a person's life. Once you were baptized, that was it; it could not be repeated or undone. A Christian group might believe only their group could *really* baptize, and so anyone who joined had to be baptized into their group even if they were already baptized somewhere else. But this is not truly re-baptism since in their eyes the first time wasn't real; nothing happened at all that first time.

There are two reasons for Christians' reluctance to perform baptism more than once. First, baptism is an initiation ritual and like most initiation rituals, it is understood to effect what it celebrates. When the president of the United States takes the oath of office, he becomes the president. The oath, in a sense, makes him president. In marriage, the "I do," the commitment, makes one married. So once you are baptized, you're a Christian. You can't join twice for the first time. There is no need to repeat the beginning. This does not mean that is it not important to renew one's marriage vows or one's baptismal vows. It is important, and we will get to that. It's just that you can't do this again for the first time, and "initiation" means "first time."

Second, baptism is, in a sense, done by God. It doesn't depend on who does the baptism. Even a nonbeliever can baptize, although it's hard to see why they would want to. As long as the person being baptized wants to be baptized (or in the case of infants, the godparents want it done for the child), it happens. Of course, as discussed above, most people actually experience God through other people's love, and this is true also for those baptized. The community welcomes them and helps them live the life they are pledged to, yet the baptism signals and effects a commitment on the part of the one baptized to let God's Spirit into their lives. Once the commitment is made, it can and must be renewed, but it can't be undone, at least from God's side or the community's side, so it doesn't need to be repeated.

So down through the centuries, rather than repeat the baptism of an infant, other ceremonies have "extended" baptism until the time when the person baptized as an infant can make their own choice and publicly renew that choice. For centuries in Western Christianity, this ceremony was confirmation. Originally a ritual of entering adulthood, there is some dispute today about the appropriate age for confirmation. In some churches, a young person is confirmed before their first participation in the Eucharist, called "first communion," around the age of seven or eight; in other places, confirmation ordinarily takes place in adolescence, around age fourteen or fifteen. There are reasons to justify either decision; perhaps there is place at both ages for a confirming liturgy[2] in which a young person baptized as an infant is given the opportunity to make a personal declaration of their choice of Christian life. In any case, it seems that the meaning of this ritual is exactly what the name indicates: after a period of experiencing what it means in practical life to be a Christian, a person can with more adult awareness repeat the baptismal commitment.

Other Christian groups do not practice confirmation, but they do require an extensive period of training before a young person's first communion. This is the opportunity for the young person to make their own the commitment to Christianity first undertaken by their parents and godparents when they were infants. In any case, there is in most Christian communities ample opportunity to renew one's baptismal vows. This occurs, for example, at most baptisms. Those gathered together are invited to renew their own vows. At most Easter services, particularly if baptisms take place during the liturgy, the entire community renews the same vows they took (or that were taken for them) the day they were baptized.

Baptism Today

Over the centuries, the baptism of infants became all too often a cultural rather than truly Christian event: in many countries any respectable Christian family was expected to have its newborn children baptized, even though there was little understanding of the ritual, its demands, and its effects. This religious event became mainly a social and even a political event. As noted above, this sadly continues to happen even today.

---

2. The word "liturgy" comes from the Greek word for "public work" (leitourgia) and is used to describe the performance of Christian rituals, especially the Sunday service.

In the sixteenth century, some of the Reformers argued that children should not be baptized. Only adults could be baptized, and then only when they were certain that they had been called to the Christian life. This remains the teaching, for instance, of the Baptists (hence their name) and of the Disciples of Christ. For these Christian groups, baptism can only be received by adults who feel that God has granted them salvation and forgiven their past sins. Baptism is a one-time, life-changing experience, a special gift of God. This is, as noted above, what the earliest Christians experienced in Pentecost. For many of these Christians, one cannot be saved without this experience and without baptism.

Most Christians, however, are still baptized when they are infants. While this ongoing practice has all the advantages of a living tradition, there are some difficulties that need to be addressed: for one thing, if ritual baptism becomes a standard practice in a culture, many people can tend to observe it as a cultural dictate rather than focusing on its deep religious meaning. It can become routine, and to some extent that happened in some countries that were traditionally Christian. In those situations it would have been unheard of that a couple did not bring their newborn children to be baptized. So, even though there was little commitment to nurturing the child's Christian faith after baptism, the child was brought to church for a short baptizing ritual. After the quick baptizing at church, the family—often a large extended family—would gather at the home for a celebration; but the religious ritual could scarcely be called a ceremony, and most of those at the home celebration were not at church for the baptizing. Similar to those who have their babies baptized out of fear of hell, these people do so as rather thoughtless social custom.

Roman Catholicism: Changes since Vatican II

In Roman Catholic circles, this decline in the actual significance for people of Christian baptism was faced at the Second Vatican Council (1962–1965) in its first major document, the *Constitution on the Sacred Liturgy*. The council's dictates for serious revision in the practice of baptizing were implemented immediately after the council by the revised *Ritual for the Christian Initiation of Adults*, commonly referred to as the *RCIA*. While this revised ritual was directed formally at Roman Catholics, since the council it has had an influence on other Christian churches as well. What this decree provides for are several things: (1) it restores the catechumenate; (2) it insists that the prime example of baptism is the baptism of an adult, though it encourages the baptism of infants and modifies the ritual to provide for this; (3) it makes clear that baptizing should be done in the presence of many, if not all, the members of the community into which the baptizand is being initiated.

The Catechumenate

The catechumenate is a several-month period of preparation for baptism of a person who intends to become a member of a Roman Catholic community. Obviously in this case one is dealing with an adult, and the catechumenate has a double purpose: (1) to instruct the person about Christian faith and life, about the mystery of Christ, the nature of the church, and the responsibilities undertaken by one who becomes Christian; and (2) to test and strengthen the purpose of the person, to see if he or she is truly making an informed and solid decision to become Christian. Obviously, in the case of infant baptism, which still remains the principal context for baptisms, the child is unable to make the personal decision of faith that is the heart of the ritual. Instead, the parents and the sponsors or godparents (people chosen to take over the responsibility of sustaining the child's faith, if something were to happen to the parents) act in the name of the child and pledge themselves to nurture the faith life of the child. In these cases of infant baptism—and in the case of the majority of Christians today who never went through the catechumenate—the process of the *RCIA* can serve as a guide for needed adult education and is being used widely in this manner.

The Decision

In the course of the catechumenate, a number of rituals allow the catechumen to express a desire for baptism. When the time comes for the actual initiation ceremony, the ritual (when it is performed as a separate action and not part of a larger ritual, e.g., the Easter Vigil) begins with the person being asked why they have presented themselves to the community. To the question "What is it that you wish?" the response is "I wish the faith," and the community agrees to continue with the ritual.

Then, before the actual water ritual, the person is anointed as a sign of being strengthened for the struggle with sin that lies ahead, and the person renounces all the temptations that would lead to a betrayal of their new Christian faith: "I renounce Satan and all Satan's works and pomps." If the baptism is occurring as part of the Easter Vigil liturgy, this renunciation is joined by the members of the community, repeating the renunciation that was made at their own baptism.

The Profession of Faith

To make clear the meaning of the baptizing that is about to take place and that will be the neophyte's (literally, "the new one," meaning a newly baptized Christian) public and symbolic profession of faith, the baptizand and the attendant community proclaim the creed that summarizes their belief. In effect, what is being symbolized is the community's sharing of its faith with the new Christian. That individual is now recognized as a member of this faith community and as such a member of the worldwide church. Then follows the actual baptizing.

The Baptizing

In ancient times, as described above, the person to be baptized descended into a pool and stood with water about shoulder high and was then ritually submerged three times. Today—and for a long time—there has been some variation in the actual baptizing. Some groups—for example, the Baptists—insist on immersion, while others, like Catholics, simply pour water on the head of the one being baptized. One way or another, the symbolism is basically the same. The baptismal water is seen to signify and actually cause the purification of the person from sin, both the evil situation into which all people are born (original sin in traditional language) and any personal sins committed before baptism. The newly baptized person, in effect, is freed from the hold that evil once had over them in the sense discussed in chapter two.

More positively, as explained above, being under the baptizing water symbolizes a mystery that links with the dying of Jesus, and coming out above the water provides a link with his resurrection. By undergoing the baptizing, the new Christian is accepting faith in Christ's saving death and resurrection. Joined with this ritual declaration of belief in Jesus as the Christ is a profession of faith in God as revealed in Jesus: at each of the three immersions (or pourings) of the person, the names of Father, Son, and Holy Spirit are spoken; the neophyte is baptized in their name and power.

Following the baptizing, the new Christian may be anointed on the forehead as a sign that he or she now shares in the Spirit possessed by the community, may be clothed in a white robe as a sign of their being transformed by grace, and may be given a lighted candle as a sign of the ministerial responsibility that they now have: to be a light to the world.

The Confirming

In Catholic adult baptisms, the anointing after baptism is replaced by the more formal confirmation anointing with chrism, a mixture of oil and balsam. This is a return to the ancient ceremony of initiation where the ritual combined what today would be called baptism, confirmation, and first communion. In those times when communities were not large and there were proportionately more bishops, it was the bishop who presided over the initiation and performed the anointing with chrism. Today, the bishop is still the ordinary minister of confirmation of those who are baptized as infants, but the authority to confirm has been extended to priests who preside at adult baptisms.

Two gestures have been traditional ways of symbolizing the giving of the Holy Spirit: anointing with blessed oil and placing one's hand on a person's head in blessing. In the present-day ritual of confirmation, these two gestures are combined: the bishop places his hand on the head of the person being confirmed and with his thumb anoints the forehead with the special blessed oil, the chrism.

Prior to the actual anointing, there is a short ritual in which the bishop questions the candidates about their knowledge of Christian belief and about the responsibilities they are undertaking as mature believers. An appropriate passage from scripture is read, and the presiding bishop gives a short homily, addressing those being confirmed and encouraging them to fulfill the pledge to live out their Christian faith.

Not all Christian groups include all of these ceremonies in a baptism or christening. Particularly, Reformed Christians emphasize the water baptism, and Eastern Orthodox Christians anoint both infants and adults before immersion and confirm both immediately after the baptism. Still, the above description of the new Roman Catholic ceremony will give a fair picture of what you would encounter in the majority of Christian baptisms.

Five Elements of Ritual

So, what is it that Christians believe happens in these initiation rituals? And how do these rituals relate to the five aspects of "sacrament" that we stressed earlier?

Hermeneutic of Experience

Through baptism, a new person has been born. As a new person, he or she is supposed to see the world in a new way, the Christian way. In fact, if there isn't a new way of looking at the world, then the new Christian has yet to grow into her or his new state of life. Paul mentioned one of these changes in the passage from Ephesians quoted above. Christians ought no longer to see people in their social ranks, poor or rich, slave or free, men or women. All are equal before God. Christians ought to look for the loving selfless response in each situation in which they find themselves. Of course, this may take some training and often strong community support. That is why Christians are initiated into a community that can over time help develop a whole new way of being in the world.

Presence

The community itself, however, is the community empowered by the Spirit of the risen Christ. One makes such a commitment to such a community because of the belief that God, working through the risen Christ and the Spirit, is present in the community of faith which the person is entering through baptism. This empowerment of the Spirit makes a life of selfless love possible. It is the fire and the wind that filled the first followers of Jesus with the courage to speak of their faith and lead many others to belief. The Spirit shared by the community is given in baptism, the marvelous Spirit whose presence creates, enlivens, and makes life one of joy. This presence most often is manifested through those around the newly baptized person: the parents who will raise their children as Christian; the sponsors or godparents who guide the new Christian in their new life; and the whole wide community of support and love, both living and dead, who make up all of those just people who have sought to do the will of God.

Maturation

Clearly, the rituals of initiation are central to the process of human maturation. Maturation is a lifetime undertaking at the heart of which are certain basic decisions a person makes. In the initiation rituals this is precisely what the baptized is doing: choosing to live out the commitment of a Christian way of life. Whether that decision is one made for one as an infant, a decision to be ratified again and again in life, or whether this is a long-contemplated decision of an adult, it should be the first important step in a true maturation of the spirit.

Service

The Christian community that now includes the newly baptized exists to be of service to people, especially the needy and oppressed. The new Christian has committed herself or himself to live as Jesus lived—to reach out to all those in pain or sorrow. The Spirit of the community of faith in which the newly baptized person now shares empowers him or her to live just such a life. In fact, it is in the living of that life that baptism comes to fruition. That is precisely how one lives up to, and into, one's baptism.

Friendship

This community of faith, the church, is not basically an organization but a gathering of friends who are united in their shared belief in God's presence and in their relation as disciples to the risen Christ. It is this gathering that welcomes their new member, providing encouragement and guidance. This is why it is so important that baptism be an initiation into a real, live, active community. It's not just a ceremony in any church, but a joyful welcoming of a new member, someone known and loved, someone eager to be an active member herself. As described in preceding sections, friendship is the central symbol of the Christian life, and it is this friendship that ought to enliven the Christian community into which one is initiated.

5

Rituals of Prayer, Worship, and the Eucharist

From the earliest records of Christianity, it is clear that Christians met frequently for community prayer. When they met for prayer, they also shared a meal. More precisely, the meal was an integral part of praying in the first century. In the First Letter to the Corinthians, Paul already describes the Christian ritual meal (and prayer service) as "traditional":

> For I received from the Lord what I also handed on to you, that the Lord Jesus on the night when he was betrayed took a loaf of bread, and when he had given thanks, he broke it and said, "This is my body that is for you. Do this in remembrance of me." In the same way he took the cup also, after supper, saying, "This cup is in the new covenant in my blood. Do this, as often as you drink it, in remembrance of me." For as often as you eat this bread and drink the cup, you proclaim the Lord's death until he comes. (1 Cor. 11:23–26)

The gospels of Mark, Matthew, and Luke give a similar account of the ritual meal (often called the "Last Supper") that Jesus held with his followers during the Passover season immediately before his death (Mark 14:22–25; Matt. 26:26–29; Luke 22:19). Many scripture scholars think that these accounts of Jesus' last meal also reflect the community celebrations of that meal, as does the account of

Jesus' appearance to followers at Emmaus while at dinner with them (Luke 24: 13–33).

Early Christian Gatherings

By the middle of the second century, the general outline of the weekly community prayer of the Christians was clear. Justin Martyr, the second-century Christian writer,[1] described this gathering as they occurred in his community in Rome:

> And on the day called Sunday, all who live in cities or in the country gather together to one place, and the memoirs of the apostles or the writings of the prophets are read, as long as time permits; then, when the reader has ceased, the president verbally instructs, and exhorts to the imitation of these good things. Then we all rise together and pray, and, as we before said, when our prayer is ended, bread and wine and water are brought, and the president in like manner offers prayers and thanksgivings, according to his ability, and the people assent, saying Amen; and there is a distribution to each, and a participation of that over which thanks have been given, and to those who are absent a portion is sent by the deacons. And they who are well to do, and willing, give what each thinks fit; and what is collected is deposited with the president, who succours the orphans and widows and those who, through sickness or any other cause, are in want, and those who are in bonds and the strangers sojourning among us, and in a word takes care of all who are in need. But Sunday is the day on which we all hold our common assembly, because it is the first day on which God, having wrought a change in the darkness and matter, made the world; and Jesus Christ our Saviour on the same day rose from the dead. (First Apology, c. 67)

Justin, like Paul and gospel writers before him, linked the ritual meal of bread and wine with the presence of the risen Christ in the community:

> And this food is called among us Eukaristia [the Eucharist], of which no one is allowed to partake but the man who believes that the

---

1. Justin was converted to Christianity around the year 130. He taught Christianity as a philosophy first in Ephesus and then in Rome. He wrote two apologies for Christianity, as well as a dialogue with the Jew, Trypho. He was martyred in Rome c. 165. An account of his martyrdom based on official court reports still survives. For more information on Justin, see note 1 in chapte 4.

things which we teach are true, and who has been washed with the washing that is for the remission of sins, and unto regeneration, and who is so living as Christ has enjoined. For not as common bread and common drink do we receive these; but in like manner as Jesus Christ our Saviour, having been made flesh by the Word of God, had both flesh and blood for our salvation, so likewise have we been taught that the food which is blessed by the prayer of his word, and from which our blood and flesh by transmutation are nourished, is the flesh and blood of that Jesus who was made flesh. For the apostles, in the memoirs composed by them, which are called Gospels, have thus delivered unto us what was enjoined upon them; that Jesus took bread, and when He had given thanks, said, "This do ye in remembrance of Me, this is My body"; and that, after the same manner, having taken the cup and given thanks, He said, "This is My blood"; and gave it to them alone. (First Apology, c. 66)

Today's Christian Gatherings

The weekly community prayer of most Christian groups today would not differ significantly from that described by Justin. Different Christian groups, however, certainly emphasize different elements of the service described by Justin. Those Christian groups who follow the sixteenth-century Reformers would put the reading of scripture and the explanation of that scripture in the central place of community prayer, so much so that the sharing of the bread and wine might not even take place or would take place rarely. Other groups, particularly the Roman Catholic and Eastern Orthodox Christians, have traditionally stressed the presence of the risen Christ in the shared bread and wine. The different names Christians have for this service (Eucharist, Mass, communion service, Lord's Supper, Sunday service, etc.) reflect these different emphases.

Each of the traditional names for this Christian ritual implies an emphasis on a particular part of the ritual. Not all groups, however, share communion every week or even every month. Some do not share communion at the weekly service at all. A few groups, notably the Society of Friends (commonly known as Quakers) may not even include readings from scripture. In order to attempt to encompass all these variations the more neutral term, "Christian community prayer or ritual" will be used in this book to avoid prejudicing the emphasis of any one Christian community.

Christian prayer, as should be clear by now, is made up of several different elements, some reaching far back in history to a very different culture from ours. Some of the expressions that Christians use to describe their community prayer hark back to this earlier time and need a careful explanation so as not to mislead even some Christians. A good place to start might be with the sharing of the bread and wine. This ritual action is included in all the early descriptions of Christian community prayer; in fact, community prayer is called "the breaking of the bread" in the Acts of the Apostles (Acts 2: 42, 46).

Christian Ritual Meals

Meals are some of the most powerful and universal of human rituals, so it is no wonder that Christians also share ritual meals and have done so from the very beginning of their movement. It is clear in all the early accounts we have of Jesus and his followers that ritual meals were an important part of their companionship. Jesus and his group are even accused of enjoying dinner parties a little too much. Jesus and his followers were, of course, Jewish, and so it was the Jewish rituals surrounding meals that formed their understanding of a ritual meal. The most important of these meals for the Jews was, and is, the Passover meal, the Seder.

In all of the accounts of Jesus' life, the last meal with his disciples, held during the Passover season, if not actually the Seder meal itself, was understood as a central moment in Jesus' life and later in the life of the community. The accounts mentioned above differ somewhat, but they agree in their accounts of that meal that Jesus identified himself with the lamb sacrificed in the Jewish temple and eaten at the Seder meal. Further, he pledged to be with his followers whenever they gathered to ritually share a meal in memory of that last night and of Jesus' anticipated death and later resurrection.

Ritual Meals and Sacrifice

For modern readers to fully grasp the significance that the memory of such a meal had for the early followers of Jesus, some basic notion of what ritual meals entailed in the first century is in order. First, ritual meals were almost always associated with sacrifices. Some sort of food was sacrificed to a god or goddess (or in the case of the Jewish religion, to the one God), and then parts of the sacrifice (parts of the animal slain, or grains of wheat or drops of wine) were offered to the deity, while the remainder of the sacrifice was eaten by the followers of the deity. Meals and sacrifices usually went together and were understood as a single ritual. Not all sacrifices entailed meals, and there were different kinds of ritual meals and sacrifices, but very often the two went together and this was certainly the case in the Passover meal.

The meaning of the ritual could be fairly complex, but, essentially, the sacrifice involved putting something aside for a sacred purpose. In order to eat the meal, of course, the animal had to be slain, but the killing was only a necessary preliminary to the meal. The deity was understood to share in the meal with those who ate the sacrificial food. The deity would really be there, sharing a meal with those devoted and willing to set aside something for that divinity.

So the ritual sacrifice/meal is essentially a prayer, but it was a prayer that was also ritual meal, a party if you like. The ritual not only united the believers with their god(s) but also united the believers themselves into a community reinforcing their beliefs and their commitment to a particular lifestyle. Often sacrifice has been seen only in a negative light; it is the irrevocable giving up of something, usually painfully. This is to miss the central point of a sacrifice/meal. Surely something was irrevocably given up, set aside, for a sacred purpose, but the central purpose of a sacrifice was celebratory and joyful—a meal with divine and human friends.

The Passover Meal

This is a rather simple picture of a complex ritual, but it will help to understand the background to the more specific Jewish ritual meal of Passover. This particular meal commemorated and commemorates the "passing over" of the houses of the Jews when the angel of death visited Egypt and killed the firstborn male of each household. In memory of this event, and of the resulting rescue of the Jews from slavery in Egypt, Jews at the time of Jesus ate a ritual meal consisting of a lamb slain in the temple, as well as other ritual foods (for instance, unleavened bread), which reminded them of their hurried escape from Egypt so long ago. Here was a sacrifice and a ritual meal joined together to commemorate the liberation of the Jewish people from slavery and to anticipate the further liberation promised by God through the coming of the "Messiah," the anointed one.

Jesus' Passover Supper

According to the accounts left to us, Jesus celebrated this ritual meal (or one during the Passover season) on the night before he died. However, he changed the usual blessing over the bread and over the wine during the meal. Jesus identified himself with the bread and wine and distributed both to his followers, instructing them to continue to celebrate this meal in his memory.

Any first-century reader, and especially any Jewish reader, of these accounts would immediately be struck by the complex symbolism. Jesus, just before his death, is associated with the sacrifice of the lambs in the temple. He inserted his coming death into the history of God's liberating relationship with the Jewish people and promised to be present to his followers whenever they met to eat this meal and remember him. For that reason, all Christian rituals, but in a special way the Christian meal, is *anamnesis* (Greek for memorial, remembrance, or commemoration); sharing the meal in memory of Jesus and all he did makes him present in this symbolic action.

It must be quickly added that the most important aspect of Jesus' death recalled and celebrated here is that it was a death of selfless love. What is essential here was not what Jesus was giving up (although some Christians have fixated on this aspect of sacrifice in the past), but why he was giving up his life and what he wished to gain by that selfless act. To give one of many possible examples, any child or spouse who gives up her career and personal life to care for a terminally ill parent or spouse knows that the essence of "sacrifice" is not what you are giving up but why you are doing so and for whom. As one of our students beautifully expressed it: "This gratuitous compassion (of such a child or spouse), this unilateral declaration of love proclaims the gospel more powerfully than bishops or theologians."[2] This, then, is a sacrifice that is celebrated: it is the cause of rejoicing that celebrates not loss but the joy of selfless love and the freedom it brings about. It is Jesus' loving intent to give himself as the source of life to his human brothers and sisters that makes him always the principal agent of the ritual and of what the ritual effects.

That is why the Eucharistic ritual has been named a "sacrifice" by many Christian groups down through history. Not that Jesus would ever die more than once, but that this meal is never divorced from the original sacrifice made by Jesus when he gave up his life. Christians never did sacrifices again, unlike most other people of the first century. Instead, they came to call their ritual meal "a sacrifice of praise" or "a thanksgiving"—in Greek, "Eucharistia" or Eucharist, as Justin Martyr, for instance, described it. The one sacrifice that Jesus made of his life would never be repeated, but it would "come to life" in

---

2. Cathleen Sanchez, "A Sacred Journey: The Role of the Primary Caregiver in the Ministry to the Sick and Dying," unpublishd paper, University of San Diego, 2003.

the ritual meal when, Christians believed, the risen Christ would be present in and with the community sharing the meal.

But again, the emphasis here should not be placed exclusively or even mainly on what Jesus gave up but, rather, on the reason he did so and on the result of that action. Early Christians understood the meal they shared as celebrating mainly the resurrection of Jesus and their own resulting salvation. Jesus freely gave his life over for a sacred purpose: he set aside his life in order that we might be saved. If this were the end of the story, there wouldn't be much to celebrate. The amazing thing, according to Christians, is that the selflessness of Jesus worked. He was raised from the dead and, even better, so would those who believed in Jesus and lived the kind of selfless life he lived. The Christian meal is a joyful celebration of the outcome of the entire process, not just a memorial of the loss and pain entailed.

Christian Commemoration of the Supper

Further, by accepting the bread and wine specially blessed by Jesus in this way, his followers agreed to "be with him," to follow his example of selflessly doing God's will. In a very powerful way, the followers of Jesus felt themselves so empowered by the presence of Jesus when they shared this meal that they became Jesus; that is, they continued the message and actions of Jesus on earth. They also believed, of course, that living such a life would entail eternal life just as it had for Jesus.

Since the followers of Jesus also understood him to be the Messiah, the anointed one promised by God to liberate God's people, they would understand this meal as commemorating Jesus' life and his death and most importantly his resurrection as saving acts of the Messiah. In fact, one of the ways in which Jesus was experienced as still alive by his early followers was in the experience of Jesus as the now risen and transformed Christ in this commemorative meal. Jesus' followers also realized that this liberation was not yet complete, and so his followers expected that, in some form or another, either in this world or in the next, Jesus would finally establish a new and perfected life. For these Christians, the ritual meal anticipated, was a "foretaste" of, a future meal with Jesus, the Messianic banquet, when all evil would finally be cured.

So from the earliest days of Christianity, the followers of Jesus would meet and share a meal in memory of Jesus. This meal carried several overlapping and related messages. Jesus is still alive and with us in community. Jesus is the Messiah and has completed the liberation begun by God in the Exodus from Egypt. Jesus has freed us from sin and from death even now, but some day we will share this meal with Jesus in perfect freedom from sin and death. The presence of the now risen Christ empowers us to the same selfless kind of life that Jesus demonstrated. By sharing this meal, we are pledging ourselves to live as Jesus did: to help the helpless, to feed the hungry, to cure the sick—in short, to reach out to all in need. This meal makes us one in this pledge, it makes us Christians, it empowers us to be the risen Christ for each other and for every one we meet.

Not that all Christians thought (or think) this every time they participate in the Christian ritual meal. Rituals just don't work like that. Powerful rituals express many things at the same time in a way more eloquent than any words will ever be able to do. In fact, for over 800 years, no Christian sat down and wrote a book just on the Lord's Supper, the Eucharist, the "breaking of the bread."

Within a relatively short period of time, the Christian meal also stopped being a real meal. The "meal" was reduced to reception of the bread and the wine over which the blessing ascribed to Jesus was recited. Almost all Christian groups today celebrate their important ritual meal by sharing only bread and wine. Some use unleavened bread (most Western Christians) and some leavened bread (most Eastern Christians), and a few use grape juice instead of wine (some churches in the Reformed tradition), but for most Christians the essential elements of the "meal" are small portions of bread and wine.

Meal and Word of God

If you attend a Christian meal ceremony, however, you will find that most Christians have a rather lengthy service that includes much more than just the sharing of bread and wine. From the earliest times, Christians also read from scripture when they gathered to share the meal. Christian scripture consists of a version of Jewish scripture, as well as a number of writings by Christians of the first and perhaps early second centuries. How this Bible came to be put together is a fascinating story, but for now it will have to suffice to state that just as first-century Jews met in a synagogue to read passages from the Jewish bible and then comment upon them, so, too, the early followers of Jesus met to read scripture and then interpret them in light of their belief that Jesus was now the risen Christ.

Of course, first-century people did not meet as we would to read a book. When we meet everyone (or nearly everyone) can read, and there are usually enough books around for everyone to have their own copy and follow along.

Not in the first century, though; first of all, books were very, very expensive to make and so a real luxury item. Animal skins had to be procured, then scraped, cured, cut, and ruled. Then you had to find someone who could write. Finally you would have to somehow convince someone to loan you the book you wanted to copy. Even if you used papyrus, a sort of paper made from reeds, it was still very expensive and time consuming to make a copy of a book.

Even more problematic was the fact that very, very few people could read or write. Those who could were highly educated and usually wealthy or the slaves of wealthy people. So when a first-century Christian group gathered, they got out a book or a part of a book that was very precious to them and then counted on an educated person from their community to read part of the book to them. Then the person who read the book, or some other teacher, would give an explanation of what the passage meant. For centuries, at least until the time of printing, this is what "reading" meant to most people. No wonder the Latin word for "a reading" is *lectio*, from which we get our word for "lecture." A person who could lecture was one who could read a book and had a book to share.

Ritual Proclamation of the Word

For those Christians in the tradition of the sixteenth-century Reformers, this reading of scripture with its accompanying explication is the great moment in prayer. Here the risen Christ, as Word of God, touches hearts and transforms them in the preaching of the good news of salvation. This is not to say sharing of the bread and wine does not also occur or that it is not important, but, rather, the central act of community prayer is clearly preaching.

An ancient tradition supports this understanding. For all the reasons given above, it would be at the weekly community prayers that most Christians learned their faith and heard scripture read. In fact, many scholars would argue that the reason the books Christians now include as part of the Christian part of the Bible (gospels, letters, etc.) were so included is because they were the books most often read at community prayer services. There were, after all, more gospels, letters, and acts attributed to the followers of Jesus than just the ones Christians use now. The early Christian communities, over time, came to choose these books mainly because they were the books which when proclaimed and explained powerfully moved the Christian community "to the imitation of these good things," as Justin Martyr so aptly put it.

Further, it was in the liturgy that those interested in becoming members of the Christian community would be trained in Christian teaching. They would be allowed to stay for the reading of scripture and for the sermon on that scripture and then asked to leave. They could not yet partake of the ritual meal, but they could be moved to repentance and membership in the community by the Word of God. In this sense, the pronouncement of scripture proceeds and makes possible the membership in the community symbolized by the sharing of bread and wine. This is the emphasis restored by the sixteenth-century Reformers and retained in those communities who continue in their tradition.

A Lived Ritual

So, at least by the second century, Christians would gather on Sunday, the traditional day when Jesus rose from the dead. Someone from the congregation would read a passage or two from the Jewish Bible, which Christians used, and from writings about Jesus. Then the passages would be explained and perhaps discussed. Only after this would the truncated meal of specially blessed bread and wine be shared. A further and important component of the ritual would be a gathering of money or food or clothing to help all those in need. This final act was understood to be as important as all the other actions for it showed that the community was serious about its commitment to continue Jesus' mission to the poor and needy.

After the meal, the blessed bread and wine was taken to those members of the community who were too sick to attend and to those in prison. Since this meal united all those to the risen Christ and to each other, it was important that all share in the ritual. In fact, in some communities, the blessed bread and wine were taken home and shared during the week by families within the community to continue to celebrate the unity that the meal entailed.

Throughout Christian history, and in all Christian denominations, community prayer has been understood as the place where Christians commit themselves anew to continue the work of Jesus on earth. Further, this work of selfless giving is enabled and empowered by the presence of the risen Christ encountered in the reading of the Word and in the shared meal. This is essentially what Christians mean when they say they are "the Body of Christ." They are now empowered to act selflessly in the world, to let the risen Christ work through them to continue his self-giving in and through the community. That is also why Christians have at times been very reluctant to share this community prayer with anyone in their community who is not at least trying to live this form of selfless life, or, to put it another way, anyone through whom the risen Christ appears not to be working. Again from earliest times, Christians have excluded egregious sinners from the community prayer and the community table. This is formally "excommunication," or exclusion from communion in the brotherhood and sisterhood that the community prayer and meal represent.

The fourth-century Christian writer Augustine of Hippo states this clearly in describing how Christians ought to understand the bread presented to them:

> "You are the body of Christ and individually members of it" (I Cor. 12:27). If, therefore, you are the body of Christ and His members, your mystery has been placed on the Lord's table, you receive your mystery. You reply "Amen" to that which you are, and by replying you consent. For you hear "The Body of Christ," and you reply "Amen." Be a member of the body of Christ that your "Amen" may be true. (Sermon 272)[3]

Unity in Diversity

Here are the essentials of what most Christians would understand as a Christian Sunday worship service: readings from scripture and a sermon, the sharing of bread and wine, and a sharing of resources to help those in need. Beyond these essentials, the Christian weekly service can differ widely from group to group. Many Christian groups meet to pray in this way more often than just on Sunday; some meet every day, in fact. Eastern Orthodox liturgies are long and formal affairs with some actions hidden from the general congregation. Great emphasis is placed on the role of the Holy Spirit in empowering the community with the presence of the risen Christ. A Baptist Sunday service might be dominated by a powerful sermon on the scripture reading, with community participation and enthusiastic singing. The vast differences that once distinguished Christian community worship services are slowly disappearing in the twenty-first century, however. Roman Catholics, Anglicans, Lutherans, and Methodists all read the same Scripture passages at Sunday worship. A Christian Sunday service might then contain some or all of the following ritual elements:

1. An entrance ritual in which the presider alone or with attendants enters the church accompanied by music, often sung by the congregation or by a professional choir

3. Quoted in Daniel J. Sheerin, *The Eucharist* (Winlmington, DE: Michael Glazier, 1986), 95.

2. A welcoming prayer
3. A penance prayer or service; this is often the formalized, "Lord, have mercy" but could even be the dramatic "altar call" where a sinner confesses his errors and repents
4. The reading of the scriptures
5. A sermon, usually explaining the scripture readings
6. Petitions for the needs of the community
7. A recitation of the creed, a formal statement of Christian belief
8. A collection of money or gifts for the support of the community
9. A second procession where the bread and wine are brought up to the celebrant
10. Prayers in praise of God's great deeds and for members of the community living and dead
11. An invocation of the Holy Spirit to make present the risen Christ
12. A repetition of the blessing spoken by Jesus over the bread and wine
13. A communion service where the blessed bread and wine are shared
14. An exit ritual, often including a recessional

Interspersed between these elements might be hymns and announcements of various kinds.

Outside this formal liturgical setting, other informal rituals, often very important to the community, also occur. Some churches welcome members as they arrive; most have some sort of gathering after the service to share food, drink, and the latest news. Usually this is coffee and donuts, but one German-American community we know used to gather every Sunday after the liturgy to share beers in the local tavern. These informal gatherings can be just as important to some members as the formal prayers as this is where the community meets to share their lives and work out the details of how the community will practically respond to the needs of its members. The informal ceremonies surrounding the formal prayers should never be underestimated. Someone who sleeps through the sermon might have an important reconciliation with a former enemy over coffee and donuts.

Problems: Real Presence

As we have already mentioned, all Christians would describe themselves as empowered by the presence of the risen Christ. Frequently, this empowerment is described as experienced in community worship. Sadly, the question of how that presence is understood has often divided Christian communities, even violently. Since these disagreements are still operative in and among Christian communities, it might be wise to describe some of these differences and how they came about.

All Christians would agree that somehow the risen Christ is present in the community and in its celebrations. Further, this presence is real in the sense that it is experienced by the Christian community as a real force in its life. If you ask most Christians, "Is Jesus a real part of your life?" you would most likely receive an enthusiastic "yes!" Christians do not mean by this that they meet Jesus walking down the street or that they call him regularly on their cell phones. They would readily admit that Jesus is no longer present to people as he was when he was alive in the first century. In short, the presence of Jesus in a Christian's life is "real" but not "physical." Jesus cannot be seen or touched or heard like other human beings we know.

The problem over the centuries has been to describe a relationship that is "real" but not "physical." This is no less difficult in the twenty-first century than it was in, say, the eleventh century. For many people, the physical is the real; if something cannot be touched or tasted or seen, it simply doesn't exist. We have discussed this problem in the introduction. For such people, symbols themselves are meaningless: flowers are always only flowers, bread is always only bread, et cetera. For such people, Christian rituals would hold no attraction in any case.

But if one is Christian and does experience the presence of the risen Christ, how can this be explained? When Christians say, as Justin Martyr did in the second century, that the bread and wine on the altar are "really" now the body and blood of Christ, what does this mean? One thing it cannot mean is that Jesus is present just as he was on earth in the first century. In fact, Christians in general have reacted against two extremes in describing how the risen Christ is present in communal ritual: a belief that somehow the risen Christ is actually physically present, and a belief that the risen Christ is present only in memory and devotion of the congregation and so is not "really" there at all.

Medieval Explanations

Starting in the eleventh century and most fervently in the later Middle Ages in western Europe, Christians emphasized the reality of this presence. The same body that Jesus had on earth was something really present in the bread and wine. This insistence was a reaction to a group called the "Cathars" ("pure ones") who denied that any physical things (bodies or bread; wine or blood) could have any spiritual value. In fact, for the Cathars, all matter was part of an evil entity that must eventually be destroyed. This insistence by Western Christians on the value of physicality led to extremes, especially in some devotional practices. Consecrated bread was stolen to make love potions. Even worse, Jews were wrongly accused of desecrating the consecrated bread, thus justifying a growing antisemitism in western Europe. Special rituals and feasts were established to honor the risen Christ present in the consecrated bread, which was displayed as a relic.

Theologians went to great lengths to explain how the body of the risen Christ present in heaven could also be present in the consecrated bread and wine. They eventually coined a term and concept, "transubstantiation," to describe how this could happen. The concept is based on Aristotelian metaphysics and claims that the "substance" or "essence" of the bread and wine consecrated in the ceremony were changed into the "substance" or "essence" of the body and blood of the risen Christ. Since "substance" cannot be sensed, but only apprehended by the mind, this explanation seemed to work, but it was a very technical theological approach, endlessly debated by theologians and understood by almost no one else.

Reformation Explanations

When Luther, Zwingli, Calvin, Cramner,[4] and others attempted to reform the western European church in the sixteenth century, they attacked this very phys-

---

4. These four men were the most famous leaders of the sixteenth-century Reformation of Christianity in Europe. Martin Luther was a doctor of theology and professor of scripture at Wittenberg in Germany, a post that he held until his death in 1546. In 1517, furious with the sale of indulgences, he proposed for discussion ninety-five theses on indulgences by posting them on the church door at Wittenberg. Immediately, his attack on the abuse of indulgences was hailed throughout Europe, and Luther was required to defend his views. Luther responded by refusing to recant and by working to reform the Catholic Church in Germany. Until his death, he was the real leader of the Reformation, translating the Bible into German, writing the catechisms and hymns that helped shape not only the Lutheran faith but also the German language.

Ulrich Zwingli was appointed to be preacher in Zurich in 1518. In 1522, he published a tract advocating the liberation of believers from bishops and the papacy. By 1525, the Mass, fasting, and clerical celibacy were banned in Zurich, and the city became the model for the Swiss Reformation. Zwingli died fighting against the Catholic Swiss in 1531.

Born in 1509, John Calvin became the spiritual and moral leader of the city of Geneva in 1541. His influence spread much wider, however, and he was the leader of the Swiss Reformation until his death in 1564. The seminary at Geneva gave refuge to many religious exiles and trained hundreds of missionaries who carried his views to Scotland, Holland, England, and France and from there all over the world.

Thomas Cranmer became a Fellow of Jesus College at the University of Cambridge in England and was ordained a priest in 1523. While in Europe, Cranmer studied the teachings of the Reformers and not only had accepted them but had married Margaret Osiander, the niece of Andreas Osiander, the Lutheran Reformer. During the reign of Henry VIII, Cranmer supported the translation of the Bible into the vernacular and was responsible for laws requiring all churches to provide this translation for their congregations. During the reign

ical understanding of the presence of the risen Christ in the communal worship service. Luther insisted on the real presence of the Christ but felt that transubstantiation was an unnecessary complication. Zwingli emphatically rejected any sort of physical or metaphysical presence of the body and blood of the risen Christ, insisting rather that the risen Christ was symbolically present and that the bread and wine remained just that, bread and wine. Christians loyal to Rome insisted equally strongly on a real presence and on transubstantiation. Calvin and Cramner tried to steer a middle course between the Romans and the Zwinglians. The result has been that the Reformed tradition of Western Christianity, following Zwingli rather than Calvin, has viewed Roman Catholics (and perhaps Lutherans and Episcopalians) as horribly deluded—if not, in fact, cannibalistic—in their insistence on the real presence of the body and blood of Christ in the consecrated bread and wine. Catholics (and some Lutherans and Episcopalians) are equally emphatic about the sacrilege of the Reformed tradition in its insistence on a "merely" symbolic presence.

After centuries of fighting and much misunderstanding, the different groups involved, sometimes hesitantly, have reached a much more tolerant position. All agree that the risen Christ somehow empowers the community and that this empowerment takes place in an important way in the communal prayer ritual. Most at least nominally recognize the value of the other traditions while adhering to their own. Yet differences still remain, and the different ways in which the different communities practice the ritual meal and the importance that they give to that meal reflect those differences.

Problems: Who Leads the Liturgy?

The various Christian communities are more seriously split over the question of who can legitimately lead the community in ritual prayer. The whole issue of community ministry is addressed in more detail in chapter 7, but fundamentally the issues revolve around what constitutes a legitimate ministry. For the Eastern Orthodox, the Roman Christians overstepped the bounds of their ministry when they claimed that the patriarch of Rome (the pope) had jurisdiction over the whole of Christianity, including the patriarchs of the Orthodox churches. Other differences also divide Roman Catholics and the Orthodox churches, but this difference affects community prayer directly. Orthodox

---

of Edward VI, Cranmer was the principle author of the Forty Articles of 1553 and the *Book of Common Prayer* of 1542. Cramner's *Book of Common Prayer* is a masterpiece of both liturgy and of the English language, forming the basis for all later editions up until modern times.

churches do not allow Roman Catholics (or other Christian groups apart from the Episcopalians) to share in the ritual meal with them. Roman Catholics go further; they claim that apart from the Orthodox, none of the other community services are even valid since those leading the liturgy have not been approved by the Roman church. Some Baptist groups also exclude all others from participation in their services, holding that they are not truly Christian. Many other Christian groups—for instance, the Lutherans—do allow other Christians to share in their service as long as they share a belief in the real presence of the risen Christ.

The practice of excluding other Christian communities from participation in community services is one of the great scandals of Christianity. Since the ritual is meant to signify and effect the unity of the community, however, it is argued that where unity does not exist, it can and should not be celebrated. Alternatively, some Christians respond that sharing the communal service together, and sharing the presence of the risen Christ, will hasten the day when Christians accept and respect each other in their differences. As yet, that much longed for day has not arrived, and Christian communities remain seriously split over who may and who may not participate in their services. This becomes even more painful when two Christians from mutually exclusively communities wish to marry, or when a Christian from one community wishes to attend the funeral of a friend or relative from another community. Different communities have worked out different ways to deal with the touchy problem of sharing services, and the regulations (and enforcement of those regulations) are in constant flux. Nevertheless, the hope that one day all Christians will be comfortable with worshipping together seems a long way off.

Informal Community Prayer

If most Christians participate in a more or less formal public gathering at least once a week which contains some or all of the elements mentioned above, this does not mean that Christians only meet to pray at these times. Numerous variations on the more formal gatherings have taken place over the centuries and continue to take place today. In fact, the line between formal and informal celebrations is constantly if often slowly changing. All the formal ceremonies of Christianity were once informal, at least in the sense of a small group gathering, in some sense, to make up a new way of celebrating who they were.

So, at most times in the past, Christians have prayed at home in family groups. This form of worship sometimes included the consecrated bread that the family took home after the Sunday service to share during the week. Bible reading, set family prayers at night, formal or informal prayers at meals, and special prayers on important family occasions may all entail prayers of more or less formality.

Sometimes Christian groups meet under the leadership of a nonordained leader to share the community meal, read scripture, or just pray together. Again, this communal prayer may simply be friends getting together to pray, or it may involve an explicit protest against the formal public liturgy of the group. Among Roman Catholics, for instance, groups meet under the leadership of married priests or women, both of whom are excluded from formal leadership of the liturgy. Quite often, such groups feel that these small settings provide a more intimate experience of the risen Christ than the larger, more formal rituals of an organized church.

Although most Christians do participate in such small groups, even if it is only the family, they sometimes disagree about the efficacy of such meetings. Is the risen Christ present in such meetings? If the Christ is present, is he present in the same way or to the same degree as he is present in the formal rituals? Since most Christians would agree that the risen Christ acts as he will, the question makes more sense when phrased in terms of the power structures of the community in question. The underlying issue here is who has the ability to mediate the presence of the risen Christ? Can any Christian do so? Or is this power delegated only to the authorized representatives of the community? If the latter is so, who can do such authorization? A more thorough discussion of this issue is found under the discussion of ministry in chapter 7.

Suffice it to say, Christians will continue to celebrate the presence of the risen Christ in both formal and informal settings—in group gatherings led by family members, friends, charismatic leaders, and the formally authorized ministers of their respective churches. As in each of these gatherings, there will be for those present the opportunity to be empowered by the presence of the risen Christ, as well as an occasion to celebrate the community's attempts to continue the work Jesus began so many centuries ago. Without this empowerment, and without this way of life, there would be no Christianity at all. In fact, the celebration is meaningless and empty without an active life of faith and love, and any human who does not celebrate the central meaning of her or his life is tragically diminished.

Five Elements of Ritual

This most frequently celebrated and central ritual of Christianity clearly bear the marks that belong to all Christian rituals.

Hermeneutic of Experience

This ritual explicitly offers Christians an opportunity to reflect on their sacred texts and to relate those texts directly to the interpretation of their daily experiences. The reading of scripture and the more or less lengthy reflection upon it make up the bulk of most Christian community prayer services. Here the minister and/or the congregation take time out of their daily lives to think back over the lives they are living and compare those lives with the kind of life they are called to live by the life, death, and resurrection of Jesus.

This can be a pretty sobering experience. How Christians actually live their lives often does not stand up to the high expectations of the Gospels. That is why most Christian community prayer services contain a penance ritual: a set of prayers and actions that acknowledge that those present have not lived up to their high calling. This ritual confession of communal and personal guilt should always take place in a setting of forgiveness, however: forgiveness both of others and of self. In fact, for many centuries, this was the ritual in which the many daily transgressions of the Christian way of life were admitted and forgiven by the community and, in Christian understanding, by God. Only for very serious and public sins was there a separate ceremony. Here was the place to honestly admit fault before God and seriously recommit oneself to the pursuit of a Christian life. A further discussion of the separate Christian rituals of reconciliation appears in chapter 8, but it should be remembered that this is the ceremony in which for centuries Christians experienced the forgiveness by God of the community and of themselves. It is still the central ritual for such an experience.

Because humans can be overwhelmed by daily life—because greed, fear, power, poverty, and wealth can all erode the commitments to a Christian life—Christians need to be reminded of whom they are called to be. They need to be first forgiven for forgetting and then challenged to remember. Finally, they are empowered to be the people they first committed to being in their baptism. Each Christian community prayer service brings Christians back to (Christian) reality. The amount of money one has, the power one can wield, the standing one has in the community—none of these is the measure of human life. Despite appearances, these are not the experiences that count. Surrounded by a community striving for the same goals, reminded of those goals by the reading and interpretation of scripture, the Christian is empowered in this ceremony to look at life in a different way: from a Christian point of view, a more mature way.

Maturation

By explicitly recalling the life, death, and resurrection of Jesus, the community prayer makes the risen Christ present to that community. This presence empowers the community to continue the work Jesus began on earth: to reach out to the marginalized people of society and to work to overcome that marginalization. Living such a life of self-giving, as we have noted, is the essence of Christian living. It is a very difficult life to live, however. Most Christians would agree that such a life is simply not possible for human beings on their own. A life of selfless love is only possible for those empowered by the risen Christ. This claim seems to run counter to the evidence that many people live such lives who are not Christian, and Christians down through the centuries had offered different ways of explaining how this could be.

For Christians, themselves, however, community prayer enables them to embrace a life which from their understanding of human life fulfills and enriches them. However this might be explained theologically, as a one-time event of salvation or as a gradual process of growth, Christians experience the community prayer service as the place where they grow in understanding of the life to which they are committed. Even more, they often find that community prayer strengthens them so that they gradually, and with fits and starts, actually begin to be the kind of people they want to be: caring, thoughtful, responsible, self-giving—in short, adults. This ceremony, more than any other that Christians celebrate, recalls them to their commitments as Christians and empowers them to live out those commitments. The ritual should be, at its best, a celebration of the desire to be fully adult and human and a ritual that empowers one to become just that.

Presence

As already described above, Christians believe that the risen Christ can be experienced in community prayer, however much they might disagree about how to describe that presence. For some, the essence of the service is the powerful word of God that touches and changes the hearts of those who truly hear it. For others, it is the real and intimate presence of the risen Christ in the reception of the consecrated bread and wine now changed into the body and blood of the Christ. What is not in doubt is that it is that presence that empowers the community. So powerfully does the risen Christ pervade the community that from the very beginning of Christianity, the community itself has been referred to as the "Body of Christ." It is in and through this community that the risen Christ continues his work on earth. That work, in its essence, is a life of selfless service.

Service

The community prayer service reminds the community of what it ought be doing and empowers the community to do it. All of this would be meaningless if the community were not living the life it is supposed to be celebrating here. That life, as has so often been said, is a life of selfless service. The form of service varies greatly. Some mainly serve their spouses, their children, their parents. Others mainly serve the larger community, either politically or socially or economically. What one cannot do is celebrate this ritual honestly and live a life only for oneself. This is a sacrilege; this is saying one thing in the ritual and quite another with one's life. Not that people don't do this, and even do it frequently. Lying is not uncommon among humans, even Christians. This is why there are prayers of reconciliation at most Christian communal prayer services.

But the point of the ceremony is to celebrate and empower a life of service. Those who take care of elderly parents at great cost to themselves, those who take lower salaries to represent the poor in court, those who do their best to provide medical care to those who can't afford it—all those who use their time, talent, and wealth to make life better for others, these are the risen Christ in action. This is what community prayer keeps telling Christians. This is what community prayer empowers them to become: "Those who say, 'I love God,' and hate their brothers or sisters, are liars; for those who do not love a brother or sister whom they have seen, cannot love God whom they have not seen. The commandment we have from him is this; those who love God must love their brothers and sisters" (1 John 4:20–21).

Friendship

As discussed at length in the section on rituals of friendship, a true friend is one who puts the needs of her or his friends above their own needs. Surely this is what the Christian community is called to do in the communal prayer ritual. The community is called to friendship, to mutual support, to forgiveness, and to compassion. In one Christian community, this call is acknowledged by their very name, the Society of Friends, most commonly known as Quakers. Christians should not only be friends to those in their own community but to those outside their community, even to their enemies.

This commitment is ritually enacted in the sharing of food. No human action is so important in establishing basic human contact as the sharing of food. In most cultures, hospitality is taken very seriously, and refusing to eat with others is a terrible insult. After absolutely stuffing oneself with wonderful food, the dread words come, "Have some more, don't you like it?" "Let's get a coffee. Let's have a drink. Would you like to go out to dinner with me some-time?" All these offers are offers not only of nourishment (or, in the case of coffee, of stimulants) but of friendship, and even of love. So when Christians eat food together, they do so with some seriousness.

As we noted sadly above, not all Christian communities will sit down and eat with others. Down through the centuries, one of the strongest sanctions the Christian community has exercised is the removal of a member of the community from the table fellowship—excommunication, literally, exclusion "from the communion." This exclusion should be occasion of great sadness within the community and exercised only with the greatest reluctance in order to bring someone to their senses, to remind them that they are not living as Christians ought. The return of the wayward Christian to the table ought as well to be the cause for great rejoicing and relief. Of course, excommunication has also been (and still is) used for political and social purposes, not to mention sheer vindictiveness, but this is not the original purpose of the practice. Christians ought to share food as friends to cement and celebrate that friendship, and only with great reluctance should any member be excluded and only as itself an act of friendship.

The most frequent Christian ritual is that of community prayer. This commonly takes the form of a reading from scripture, an explanation of that reading, and of a ritual meal of token amounts of bread and wine. Other prayers and ceremonies may or may not be interspersed with these central actions.

Christians have been meeting for this form of prayer since the very earliest days. They do so to remind themselves of who they are, of what they believe, and of the kind of life to which they are committed. They feel empowered by the presence of the risen Christ to renew their attempts to live a selfless life, just as Jesus did while on earth. So strongly is this felt that the community itself becomes the "Body of Christ" active on earth. Further, this ceremony celebrates the active life of selfless love to which the community aspires. There is probably no other ritual so central to the everyday life of the majority of Christians.

6

Rituals of Reconciliation

Beginning with Jesus' earliest disciples, Christianity has always dealt with the need for people to be reconciled. In greater or lesser ways, we humans manage to hurt one another, to strain or even break the relationships we have with one another. As a result, there is a rather constant task of healing our relationships with one another, as individuals and as groups.

Prevalence of Alienation

It is interesting that both sociologists and the Bible use the word "alienation" in describing the distancing of people from one another, and the Bible extends this to describe the break in the relationship of humans with God. We are familiar, of course, with the alienations that plague our society: racial tensions between various segments of society, misunderstandings and conflicts between nations or between ethnic groups in any particular nation, the generational gap that is so pronounced today, and the perennial "war of the sexes" that is rooted in patriarchal domination of women.

We are more aware than before, thanks to modern advances in psychology, that each of us is to some extent alienated from the person she or he could and should become. While we need not become obsessed with our shortcomings, an honest look at ourselves makes it clear that we still face the need to improve and grow as persons. If such failings are serious and deliberate—above all, if they involve harming others—we call this "sin." And Christianity has always realized that these alienations in some way damage or at times break our relationships with God. Certainly, God is beyond any harm from us, and we speak about our sins "offending God" because we sense that our human sins involve a refusal to recognize God's concern for each of us.

Jesus' Ministry of Reconciliation

But Christianity has also recognized that the breaches in our relationship to one another and to God can be healed; reconciliation is possible if we make the decision to heal ourselves as individuals and our dealings with one another. This realistic Christian admission of the need and the possibility of reconciliation began as early as Jesus' disciples' experience of Jesus' public ministry and then their memory of him. The gospel narratives of Jesus' activity during his public ministry tell of his healing lepers, so that they might become once more a part of accepted society. They contain also the touching account of his healing the woman whose continuing menstruation made her "unclean" and unable to associate with others in public. Most importantly, they witness to the way in which Jesus claimed the authority to forgive sin and the wonder works he performed to justify that claim.

St. Paul's letters focus on reconciliation as the heart of Jesus' saving work. In particular, he describes the effect of Jesus' dying and rising as a reconciliation of humans with God. However, he goes deeper and he sees at the root of this reconciling action the creative activity of God's own Spirit. What humans do to bring about reconciliation is important and necessary, but the ultimate power of reconciliation belongs to God; human reconciliation is a symbol of the divine reconciliation. Another way to say this is to say that reconciliation is a sacrament.

Common Rituals of Reconciliation

Like other sacramental areas, there are rituals that express and help effect reconciliation. Precisely because there are so many occasions where reconciliation is needed and takes place, there are manifold rituals that have been used and are still used. Most of these are "unofficial"; they are gestures that people use almost instinctively. We often refer to friends' "kissing and making up." There is universal recognition of enmity being ended by a handshake. Even in international affairs, the ending of long-standing hatreds and even war are celebrated by the leaders of opposed nations publicly shaking hands. This happened, for example, when the peace arrangements mediated by President Bill Clinton between Israelis and Palestinians was formalized in a handshake by Israeli Prime Minister Yitzhak Rabin and Palestinian President Yasser Arafat.

Perhaps the most common ritual of reconciliation is the sharing of a meal. Worldwide, to eat together is a symbol of union among people; and if these people had previously been at odds and perhaps harming one another, the shared meal clearly says that they regret this and wish the alienation to cease. Ancient Israel incorporated this symbol into the ritual of the Jerusalem temple: perhaps the most important "sacrifice" carried out in the temple was the "peace offering." In this ceremony the action symbolized a meal being shared by Yahweh and the people, a meal of reconciliation between God and the people that once more confirmed union and peace between them.

Public Ceremonies of Reconciliation

In the history of Christianity there have been several "official" sacramental rituals that have been used to symbolize and bring about reconciliation among people and reconciliation of sinners with God. Of course, the most important early celebration of reconciliation with God was baptism. By being baptized, a person gave up their earlier life of sin and committed herself or himself to a new life, one empowered by the Spirit of the risen Christ. Very early on, however, the problem arose of people who did not live up to the commitment they made at baptism. Although it was not supposed to happen, there were Christians who committed public acts that clearly were not "Christian."

Exomologesis

There is a reference as early as Matthew 18:18 that lets us know there was discussion about reconciling a member of the community who was a source of division, but no indication about the manner in which this was to happen. In a short time a process, given the untranslatable name *exomologesis*, came to be the common ritual.

The three most serious of these sins were to give up the faith in face of persecution (apostasy), adultery, and murder (the latter included taking part in judicial proceedings leading to capital punishment or killing another person in battle as a soldier). The sinner had to come before the community gathered under the presidency of the bishop and acknowledge her or his guilt. At that point the bishop, in the name of the community, imposed a penance—and they were real penances, such as ten years of fasting and exclusion from full participation in the Eucharist. Only when the penance was completed would the penitent again come before the community, usually during Holy Week, and would be solemnly reconciled. The *exomologesis* remained the central ritual of reconciliation for almost a millennium but was then replaced by a quite different ritual.

Confessional Rituals

This "new" ritual came from Ireland to the continent in Europe around the sixth century and was initially criticized by church officials as an innovation, but by the twelfth century it became the regular and officially accepted ritual. This is the ritual with which Roman Catholics in the West are familiar. In this ritual, the person privately confesses his or her sins to an ordained priest, is then absolved by the priest as a representative of the church, and receives a penance—usually some prayers to be recited after the confession. (We describe this practice a little later in this chapter.)

Currently, few Christian groups have a public penance ritual. Some Reformed churches have a ritual "altar call" after a powerful sermon. This can be a time for people to come forward publicly to proclaim their faith in the risen Lord (if they are unbaptized) or to reaffirm that faith (if they are already baptized). An altar call might well include a confession of past sins that the person wishes to publicly reject. It is strongly recommended that a person who makes this emotional and difficult commitment then be counseled by qualified believers. This should lead to baptism or to a recommitted Christian life.

Several Christian groups have public prayer ceremonies, often as part of the Sunday liturgy and most particularly during Lent, when the community prays for forgiveness of sins. No one publicly confesses their sins, but the congregation is urged to think of those areas where they have not been faithful to commitments they made at baptism. This is probably the most common form of public confession in Christian practice.

Christians might do well to think seriously about reviving some form of public confession ritual. Particularly when communities are torn apart by internal strife, or when some members of the community have done great damage to the community and wish to make amends, a public ceremony can go a long way to begin to heal wounds. The Truth and Reconciliation Commission

in South Africa and the Chilean National Commission on Truth and Reconciliation are two national attempts to provide forums for healing large-scale
ruptures of human relationships. These commissions, of course, are far more
than rituals. They provide a forum to adjudicate blame, to provide closure for
the families of those injured or killed, and also to allow the perpetrators of
violence to face their victims and ask forgiveness. However, they are also powerful symbols to all concerned that the community wishes to slowly heal great
wounds, to comfort those afflicted, and to forgive those who ask for forgiveness.
It is a difficult process but far more healthy than leaving unresolved hatred
and animosity to seethe beneath the surface of the community only to reappear
again and again in new eruptions of violence.

One can imagine that rituals of reconciliation would be very helpful in
several community situations. When a corporation or government agency deliberately or accidentally harms a community through toxic waste dumping or
improper safety procedures, public forums to resolve these issues might include rituals of reconciliation. They may be no more than a handshake between
representatives of the different groups, but some form of community recognition is important so that healing can begin. Of course, this is assuming that,
first, there is an admission of guilt and, second, a sincere effort is made to
right the wrongs inflicted. Otherwise any efforts at reconciliation would be
seen as insincere.

From small community infractions like price gouging at a local store to
large national problems like the Enron scandal, public ceremonies of reconciliation coupled with a sincere attempt to right the wrongs committed can go
a long way to begin to heal community wounds. Christians, among other
groups, can offer a venue for such public rituals.

Penance

This brings us to an important part of reconciliation. It is not just enough to
say that you are sorry. Lately, public figures have taken to claiming "full responsibility" for decisions they have made without the least attempt to also
assume responsibility for the effects of those decisions. This is empty rhetoric
with no real intention of reaching reconciliation.

Christians have long asserted that it is true repentance that forgives sins.
As soon as a person is truly sorry for the damage they have caused in human
relationships, God forgives them. The problem with this teaching, as comfort-
ing as it may be, remains that the people need also to be forgiven by those

around them and by themselves. In fact, the most dramatic symbol of God's forgiveness is often the forgiveness by the community that then makes possible self-forgiveness.

Unlike God, however, humans need some assurance that those asking forgiveness are really sorry. The very best way to prove one is sorry, of course, is try to right the wrong committed. How often have we pleaded with others, "No, really, I will make it up to you; you'll see." When our friends hear this, and more importantly see a sincere attempt to make amends, then it is incumbent on them to accept us back into their friendship. In Christianity, a task was usually assigned to the person asking forgiveness in order to prove that they were really sorry. This task is called a "penance." The penance can be severe (for instance, going on a pilgrimage to a far place) or light (as in saying a few prayers). However, some task is required to prove to the community that one really is sorry. Of course, this penance does not take the place of also undoing the wrong done when that is possible.

This practice not only has the advantage of proving to the community that one is truly sorry but also allows the person who has offended the community to prove themselves: to show to themselves that they can be better people, to prove their own self-worth. It is often much harder for people to accept forgiveness and to forgive themselves than it is for others to forgive them. So many people suffer in despair, feeling that they can never be forgiven either by others or by God. Yet the only person who has not forgiven herself or himself is that person. A public confession and the performance of a penance can help a person let their sins go. By the community accepting their forgiveness, they can believe God has forgiven them and, by doing something to show their sincerity, hopefully, they can eventually forgive themselves.

Private Confession

As already mentioned, the practice of public confession and reconciliation was replaced in the twelfth century in Western Christianity with a form of private confession and reconciliation. Rather than confessing serious and public sins and performing a public penance, a form of private "spiritual direction" became the norm. At least once a year, each Christian was to confess privately all their wrongdoings, large or small, to the local minister, who would then assign them a penance commensurate with their sins. The penance would be performed privately. Usually confession took place before Easter as an attempt to recommit oneself to the Christian life in preparation for the great feast of the resurrection of Christ. The practice arose in Celtic countries, where monks would listen to the problems of the people and assign penances (sometimes quite harsh) for the sins that were confessed.

The idea seems to be that at least once a year, Christians would make a sincere attempt to reform their lives in those areas where they felt they were not living up to a true Christian life. They would confess their sins, thereby admitting that they had faults, and then, at least in the best of circumstances, the minister would counsel them on how to better live out their Christian commitment. Finally, the minister would give the penitent a penance to demonstrate their commitment to change. This was the usual ritual of reconciliation from roughly the twelfth to the sixteenth century. After the twelfth century, the minister of this ritual was always a priest. Before that, abbots and abbesses would hear the confessions of the monks or nuns under their charge, and sometime even laypeople would hear each other's confessions. Some dramatic instances of public penance, usually undertaken by political leaders, still took place, but by and large, private confession to your local priest was the rule.

Both Luther and Calvin objected to any idea that the priest or minister could forgive sin. Only God could forgive sin and justify human beings before God. Therefore, they were both careful to point out that private confession did not absolve sin and that penance did not gain people any merit in the sight of God. Lutherans still continued to practice private confession, while Calvinist churches did not. Today, private confession is limited mostly to the Roman Catholic Christians.

Reconciliation in the Roman Catholic Church

Roman Catholic Christians were the only ones to retain the frequent use of the reconciliation ritual apart from the prayers for forgiveness included in the Sunday liturgy. Like other rituals in that community, however, the practice of private confession was examined and somewhat altered after the Second Vatican Council. There now are three accepted forms of the ritual of reconciliation. The first of these is simply a continuation of what has existed for centuries, but there is greater recognition that for most people there is probably no question of grave sin to be confessed and the role of the confessor is to help people overcome lesser faults that prevent them from coming closer to God. In the second form of the ritual, there is a gathering of the community for a liturgy that expresses their shared need for reconciliation with God, their gratitude for God's forgiveness, and their resolve to work against whatever alienates them from one another and from God. This is then followed by the opportunity of private confession for those who wish it.

The third ritual is like the second, except that the liturgy celebrated by the community does not end with private confessions but with the presider giving a general absolution. For the most part, this third form of reconciliation with its general absolution is reserved for "emergencies"—for example, before the Eucharist at Christmas when there are not enough ordained confessors to provide private confession for large numbers of penitents.

Most recently, even among Roman Catholics, participation in the ritual of private confession is declining, particularly among younger people. There are some indications that we are in the midst of a major shift in the ritual celebration of reconciliation. A greater number of people see themselves as responsible only to God for their sins. On the one hand, some people see no reason for confession or ritual reconciliation with the community, especially for minor faults. On the other hand, some people seem to be more aware of the need for public reconciliation within and between communities and nations. The future of Christian rituals of initiation at present is unclear, but the need for people to accept each other and themselves even after they have committed grave offenses remains central to human relations. Some forms of Christian rituals of reconciliation will almost certainly continue.

The Five Elements

Hermeneutic of Experience

Any ritual of reconciliation contains within itself a particular way of understanding the world. Rather than a cruel and unforgiving place, the world is understood as one that allows for mistakes. So you get a second chance. When asked by his followers how often they should forgive others, Jesus responded seventy times seven times (Matt. 18:22). Jesus did not literally mean that the four-hundred-and-ninety-first time one made a mistake, that was it. This was not a "491 strikes and you're out" law. No, Jesus meant that we should *always* forgive others as God always forgives us. Every time we participate in a ritual of reconciliation, we learn the Christian world is one of constant forgiveness: forgiveness by God, forgiveness by and of the community, and forgiveness of and by ourselves.

In addition, rituals of reconciliation teach us that there is sin in the world and sin in us. Part of the ritual is the acceptance of the evil we have done as evil. Part of the ritual, too, has traditionally included an effort to show we are sorry for that wrong by attempting to reverse the effect of evil. Rituals of reconciliation should teach us not only love but also humility.

Presence

Whenever the community gathers to offer forgiveness, it is really offering the forgiveness of God as well. As explained early in chapter one in this volume, God is present to us mainly in and through other people. The loving God proclaimed by Jesus is no more powerfully present than in a ritual of reconciliation. We experience the love of God through the love of the Christian community that constantly forgives us, constantly accepts us back, and constantly reaffirms our own worth. Jesus came to save sinners, and it is precisely because we are sinners that we participate in rituals of reconciliation and through those rituals experience the presence and power of a forgiving and loving God.

Maturation

Though we always need to face the reality of our human sin, we are conscious that honestly facing our failings and repairing whatever damage we have done to others or to ourselves is part of the process of maturation. We have become more aware that much of the evil that harms persons is the result of forces in society, of alienations and prejudices and exploitation that we must address as *communities* in cooperation with one another. In such community efforts appropriate rituals are a powerful help.

On the individual level, we learn first that we too are sinners. We too are in need of the forgiveness of God and of others. We have no right to look down on others, given our own failings and need for forgiveness. To believe that we do not need forgiveness is to remain immature and probably pretty obnoxious. In contrast, nothing we can do is unforgivable as long as we recognize and accept what we have done and ask God and the community for forgiveness. No one is beyond the love of God, even if a person no longer loves himself or herself. Christians reach out to those in despair and assure through the ritual actions that they are forgiven and should therefore forgive themselves.

Service

At first glance, it might seem that reconciliation has little to do with service. First glances, however, are sometimes deceiving, and that is certainly the case here. First of all, the identification of evil is itself a service. One cannot begin to eliminate some great evil until it is first identified as evil. Second, rituals of reconciliation go further and offer an opportunity for people to admit their participation in evil and begin to make an honest effort to end that participation. Part of that commitment, as we have noted, includes a sincere attempt to undo the evil committed. Such attempts are great acts of service in themselves. Finally, one of the greatest gifts one can offer is forgiveness, and one of the greatest services one can perform for oneself and others is to accept the forgiveness offered. From these perspectives, reconciliation is essential to the continued service to which Christian commit themselves—that is, to the identification and eradication of evil in the world and in their own lives.

Friendship

As noted above, one of the greatest gifts one can offer another is forgiveness. Such an action is central to a maturing friendship. Sooner or later friends let each other down or at least are perceived to have done so. At that point, either a true reconciliation takes place or the friendship slowly (or quickly) comes to an end. This is particularly true for families. Forgiveness and reconciliation take place continuously between partners, between children and parents, and among siblings. The acceptance of one other even after the shocking recognition that the beloved is not perfect does wonders for friendship. One realizes that one is loved even though they have failed as a friend, even failed miserably.

One realizes that it is not the stunning good looks, fabulous wealth, and charming personality one thought one had that your friends find irresistible. No, your friends continue to like you when the Botox wears off, your great job has been outsourced, and you are about at prickly as porcupine knitting in a thorn tree. Your friends may tell you off, they may tell you to get a grip, but they also hang in there with you through betrayal and addiction and self-pity. Best of all, when you do come around and beg their forgiveness, knowing full well that you don't deserve it, you get it anyway. What more powerful experience can one have of the friendship of God?

7

Rituals of Service and Ministry

Organized Anything, Even Religion

More and more commonly one hears people say that they are spiritual but not religious. Usually these people mean that they feel drawn to God in some form and that they pray in some manner, but that they do not like to belong to any organized religion. They have their private beliefs but feel uncomfortable attending a church or belonging to a congregation.

When asked why this is so, many people say that organizations are too formal, too worldly, too corrupt, too self-serving. They don't want to give their money or time to an organization that does not meet their needs, does not quite fit their beliefs, and appears to be hypocritical to boot. While it is true that large organizations often seem to exist simply to perpetuate themselves and that corruption in politics, business, and, sadly, religion has dominated the headlines in the last few decades, still something can be said for organization, even for organized religion.

First, organization seems inevitable. Human beings just seem programmed to organize themselves as soon as more than two or three come together in a group. There is a good reason for this. Groups of people can do things more effectively than individuals. Ask yourself if you would prefer to make your own clothes, grow your own food, provide your own electricity, build your own house, and manufacture your own car. While you're at it, you could write your own book on Christian ritual. Or you could do your own job, get paid—and then go buy clothes and food, pay your electric bill, pay your mortgage or rent, and make payments on your car . . . and of course buy this book. Most people who say they despise organizations would still gladly take the second option here. People can then concentrate on one job and do it well while counting on other people to do their jobs well. Each of us, hopefully, gets very good at what we do, and no one needs to know how to do everything.

Most of the time this works pretty well. Organizations and bureaucracies, alas, are usually only noticed when they don't work well. People don't call the car company and thank them when their car starts day after day without a problem, but the day the car doesn't start, most people will immediately (and not unjustly perhaps) complain. The same is true for the roads the cars run on, the gas stations that provide fuel, the stoplights, stop signs, speed limits, traffic police, licensing agencies—all the "bureaucracies" that keep things running smoothly. We take them for granted and really only notice them when they aren't working. The thought has probably not occurred to most people in the United States that even having a car to drive, much less all the infrastructures necessary to drive around relatively easily, is an extraordinary privilege. None of this just happens; it only appears "natural."

Organized Religion

Organized religion in this sense is no different from organized anything. If your daughter wants a church wedding, there has to be a church. Someone has to pay to build the church, keep it up, pay the minister, light the candles, and (most important) make sure the building isn't double booked. What is more central to the Christian life, nationally and internationally, is that organized religious groups can (and do) rush aid to areas that need it more quickly and efficiently than most governments can. All this takes organization: warehouses of supplies, a network of contacts, fund-raising, and people on the spot who are part of the community. The largest processor of refugees to the United States, for instance, is the Roman Catholic Church.

In addition, there is the touchy issue of standards. Who says who is a Christian? Any one can (and does) stand up and proclaim himself or herself as a Christian and even as a Christian leader. Do all these people have an equal right to that claim? Should, for instance, Christian communities worldwide welcome Ernest Norman as the reincarnation of Jesus? Or accept his wife as the reincarnation of Mary Magdalene (as well as the reincarnation of Socrates, Peter the Great, Charlemagne, Queen Elizabeth I, Queen Maria Theresa, Hatshepsut, Akbar of India, Quetzalcoatl, and Atahualpa)? This is the claim of the Unarius Academy of Science, founded by Ernest and Ruth Norman. Their followers would claim that they are the true inheritors of Christianity and that other Christians will eventually realize this when at least thirty-three crystal spaceships arrive, interlock, and form the World Academy in sixty-seven acres of land outside of San Diego, California.

Most Christians, even those who are spiritual but not religious, would definitely reject these claims. There is nothing to support these claims in our scripture, they might say, nor in our tradition, nor in our liturgy. This is just not an acceptable interpretation of Christianity for the vast majority of Christians. The criteria for this decision are all based on centuries of organization. Out of all the books that claimed to be about Jesus written in the early years of Christianity, the majority of Christian communities agreed to use only the books which now make up the New Testament of Christianity. Given all the possible ways of praying, the majority of Christians chose the rituals described in this book with surprising uniformity of practice. Christians generally look to the same principles of action based on these books, on this liturgy, and on a long tradition of struggling to carry out those principles that make up the greater part of Christian tradition.

Tradition, liturgy, and scripture don't just happen. It takes organization to pick certain books, make sure they are regularly copied and distributed, then read and commented upon. It takes organization to regularly perform complex rituals at set times over centuries. It takes a dedicated and well-trained leadership to learn the scriptures, rituals, and traditions of Christianity and constantly call the community to remember and live up to Christian ideals. It takes an organization for any way of life, or indeed, any idea, to continue to exist over time. Organizations keep movements alive even while they radically alter them simply by organizing them. Christians, therefore, need organizations and trained leaders to remain honest to their own history and standards at the same time as those organizations help to shape that history and those standards.

Most Christian groups, for instance, have become pretty fussy about their leaders. They expect them to attend special schools where they train for service to the community. Then most Christian groups expect that prospective ministers undergo a ceremony that certifies them as legitimate leaders—an "ordination." Finally, the community appoints these new leaders ("calls" them) for a particular service to a particular community. Different groups do this in different ways, but most have strict standards that they expect of their leaders. Not just anyone can claim to properly understand and teach Christianity, at least within the vast majority of Christian communities.

This has the great advantage of curtailing a good deal of self-delusion. Although one cannot be sure, one suspects that Ernest and Ruth Norman would have had a hard time getting through seminary and even a harder time getting ordained, given their beliefs. This can be construed as prejudice (and would be by those who follow the Normans), but the majority of Christians would probably see it as quality control. Organizations develop and require standards after years and even centuries of experience. Some voices are prophetic and some are deluded, and organizations help discern the difference. In fact, this may be one reason why being "spiritual" rather than "religious" is so popular. As long as you don't have to answer to anyone but yourself, your ideas will ordinarily seem pure and even brilliant. Some people have the unusual and uncanny ability to critique themselves, many more people think they have this ability, but most find themselves to be their own best fan club. Organizations keep individuals honest. When the minister or priest gives a homily that contradicts your own views of yourself or life, you have to think again. Maybe you are just fooling yourself. Maybe Jesus wouldn't drive a Hummer after all. Nothing promotes honesty like having people around you who politely and constructively disagree. It's maddening, it's time consuming, it's hard on the ego, but it certainly is good for mature growth. People who are "spiritual" but not "religious" can miss all that. For maturity, it would seem, people need criteria against which they can judge themselves, and organized religion, despite all its drawbacks, exists in large part to provide those criteria.

The actual ritual used to celebrate the entry of a person into service to the Christian community is pretty simple and straightforward. Most often it simply entails the laying on of hands after the proper preparation. However, just understanding this ritual will hardly explain the many different forms of ministry Christians have devised and the bitter fights that have arisen over different Christian understandings of authority. In this chapter we attempt to untangle some of the background to this wrangling. Therefore, the reader is asked to be patient with what will seem like a great deal of history rather than a discussion of ritual. The patience will be worth it if the reader arrives at a better understanding of why Christians are often so bitterly divided over questions of authority—that is, over who gets to minister to the community.

In the Beginning

Most scholars of the earliest years of Christianity would agree that Jesus had no intention of founding a "church." Christianity was a way of life—in fact, a way of life within Judaism. As the movement began to grow, however, the inevitable impulse to organize manifested itself. Already by the time that the Gospels were written, certain authority figures had emerged. Some of these groups continued to have a role in Christianity, although in a much modified way, down through Christian history. Others played a more transitory part. The Twelve, a group of Jesus' closest followers, for instance, would be described by most scripture scholars as a unique group. They had no successors, at least in the sense that there was any other "Twelve" that continued on in Christian history. In fact, the listing of the Twelve by Mark, Matthew, and Luke may be more symbolic than institutional. The list of the Twelve even differs slightly in Luke from that found in Matthew and Mark. Luke does not include Thaddeus but, rather, adds a second person named Judas (not the Judas who betrayed Jesus). Most scripture scholars would argue that the number twelve was important for early Jewish Christians as a sign that Jesus was reaching out to and restoring the twelve tribes of Israel. Later it became very important that Christian communities trace their origins back to these twelve students of Jesus. "Apostolicity" became a sign of authenticity of a Christian community, although again, that will be a criterion understood differently by different communities.

Apostolicity

"Apostolicity" became attached to the Twelve who are often, in fact, called the Twelve Apostles. This can be misleading. The world *apostolos* in Greek meant "messenger" or perhaps more accurately in this context, "missionary." This term is used in the letters of the missionary Paul even before the Gospels were written. Many other missionaries are named in scripture beside the Twelve, most famously, of course, the missionary Paul. The Twelve are certainly described in Christian tradition as missionaries, but being a missionary, that is, an apostle would not be the same as being one of the Twelve. Down through history, however, these two roles have been confused, so that it is common for Christians to speak of the "Twelve Apostles" as if "the Twelve" and "Apostle" were the same thing. As least in the earlier years of Christianity, they clearly were not.

One of the problems here is translation. If translations of scripture simply took the Greek word *apostolos* and translated it as "missionary" (for instance, in English) people would know right away that there were more than twelve missionaries in the history of Christianity. As it is, the fairly straightforward Greek word *apostolos* became the esoteric English world "apostle," a word used mainly by Christians and then only to refer to a few of the early Christian leaders. This is not the only "mystification" of language that takes place when the Greek of the Christian scripture is translated into other languages. Both men and women are called *apostolos* in the letters of Paul, so we know that there were women missionaries early on in the history of Christianity.

Another term used for the followers of Jesus in Christian scripture is the Greek word *discipolos*. The word means "follower" or perhaps better "student." Jesus had lots of students, men and women, as particularly the Gospel of Luke makes clear. So in Christian scriptures, Jesus' closest followers were termed either the Twelve missionaries or the Twelve, or missionaries, or students. Since many of them actually knew Jesus, their teaching was preserved, in turn, by their students and carried particular authority. Paul, for instance, who did not know Jesus, had to justify his own missionary efforts. He did so by claiming that Jesus appeared personally to him in a miraculous event. Of course, it must be stressed that Christians believed Jesus was still alive and active in the community as the risen Christ. So even those who did not know Jesus during his active ministry could still claim to know him and have been taught by him in his new existence as the risen Christ. The prophets, for instance, were a group with great authority, particularly in Syria, where they may have been the leaders of the weekly liturgy.

None of the leadership roles of the first century were firmly institutionalized, and there seems to have been a great deal of diversity in the way groups structured themselves. As time went on, need for a more permanent and reliable organization was felt to be more and more urgent. First of all, Jesus did not immediately return to earth to establish a reign of peace, as many of his followers expected. Jesus' students were dying, and some way was needed to preserve the authentic teaching they received from Jesus. Many people who didn't know Jesus were claiming that they had a secret knowledge from Jesus not available to the followers of Jesus. In order to counter these claims and to try to preserve the original message of Jesus, an organization slowly emerged.

Christianity Becomes Organized

This process was slow and developed differently in different places. Further, the process was inevitably political and sometime nasty. Scholars still debate, in a way only scholars would, whether it would have been better if the Marcionites or the Montanists[1] had been accepted by the larger Christian community. Perhaps these groups were unjustly treated by other communities, or perhaps modern scholars are just reading their own ideas of toleration back into history. Whatever could or should have happened, what did happen was that Christians began to look for criteria by which they could determine who had the "true" teaching of Jesus. This search still goes on, of course, and one criterion still used depends on a proper recognition of ministry and authority.

When Christians did organize and began looking for structures of service and ministry, they naturally adopted the structures around them. So, not surprisingly, at least one form of organization was simply a continuation of Jewish practice. Some Christian communities continued to follow the synagogue practice of choosing elders to take care of the needs of the community and teachers (rabbis) to read scripture and comment upon it. The word in Greek for "elder" was *presbyteros*, and so from early on, Christian leaders were called presbyters, a word which eventually became "prester" and then "priest" in English. The great sixteenth-century scripture scholar and Reformer John Calvin urged a return to this early form of leadership, and particularly in Great Britain, the followers of Calvin became known as "Presbyterians," or those who have presbyters, elders, as their leaders. In this form of early ministry, a group of people, chosen by the community for their seniority and uprightness of life lead the community in prayer and supervise service to the community.

Other Christian groups followed a secular model of governance and called their leaders by the Greek title of *episcopos*. This word simply means "manager" or "supervisor." Both the Greek and the Latin literally mean one who "sees" (*scopos, visor*) "over" (*epi, super*). This title would be used for a mayor of a town, for the manager of a mine, or for the supervisor of a large plantation. The English words "biscop" and then "bishop" come from this Greek word. Since Calvin judged this development to be a later and secular practice, Presbyterians do not have bishops. In contradistinction, the term "Episcopalian" referred, again mostly in Great Britain, to those Christians who do have bishops as well as presbyters or priests. When in capitals, "Episcopalian" refers to Christian communities linked historically and in communion with the Anglican Church.

---

1. These were two early Christian movements that were understood to be heretical by most early Christian leaders. The Marcionites rejected the writings of the Old Testament and taught that Christ was not the Son of the God of the Jews, but the Son of the good God, who was different from the God of the Ancient Covenant. Montanists believed that the ecstatic prophecies of the second-century prophets, Montanus, Prisca, and Maximillia, were direct revelations of the Holy Spirit. Montanists expected the end of the world to come immediately, and they encouraged ecstatic prophesying and strict asceticism. They believed that a Christian fallen from grace could never be redeemed. Since almost all our information about these groups comes from their enemies, some scholars have suggested that the label of heretic was more political than religious.

In lowercase, "episcopalian" might refer to any of the Christian communities that have bishops (e.g., Lutheran, Roman Catholic, Orthodox), as well as "Episcopalians" proper. In this form of government, one person is chosen to lead the community in prayer and direct the charitable services central to the Christian way of life.

Another common term used in the early years of Christianity was *diakonos* or deacon. In Greek this word means "servant," and these were the people who did the everyday tasks needed by the community. They were responsible for taking care of the poor, visiting those in prison, and generally making sure the community needs were met. Like the offices of *presbyteros* and *episcopos*, the office of *diakonos* continues down to the present day, and you can find deacons playing an important role in most Christian communities.

These three offices (*episcopos, presbyteros,* and *diaconos*) provide a form of historical continuity in Christian tradition. Despite many sometimes drastic changes in both their roles and the understanding of those roles in the community, one meets these three ministries in different guises fairly consistently down through the 2,000 years of Christian history.

Although this brief introduction gives the impression that presbyteral and episcopal forms of governance were quite separate and distinct organizing principals in different communities, in fact both forms of organization could, and did, exist in the same community. One of the presbyters could be called *episcopos*, or the terms could even be used interchangeably. What was expected of both presbyters and *episcopos* was roughly the same, however. First and foremost, they were to be servants to their own communities: that is, they were to provide services for the community, rather than rule over them.

Emergence of the Episcopate

For the organization, there would need to be a person learned in the traditions and message of the *apostolos*, either directly or through others who had themselves known the first missionaries. The great *episcopos* Polycarp of Smyrna in Turkey could refute a self-appointed Christian teacher by simply relating how as a youngster he had heard John teach, thereby pointing out that "this faker" had it wrong: John never taught what the faker claimed. Of course, Polycarp had been a Christian for eighty-six years and was one of the last alive to have heard John preach. By the middle of the second century, few Christians could claim to have heard John, but they could claim they had heard Polycarp preach. This claim to be in a direct line of teachers right back to Jesus himself became an important criterion for the authenticity of the teaching of a particular community. Some communities kept lists of all the teachers in that community back to Jesus, and in a few places, particularly in Rome, these lists are very important, since they are used to prove the legitimacy and authenticity of the present *episcopos* of that community—in the case of Rome, of the pope.

In this way, Christian *episcopos* in particular became the living bearers of the tradition. Possibly also they would have been chosen not only because they could remember the tradition but also because they could read the writings of the followers of Jesus. Few people could read or write, so it would be essential that at least someone in the community be able to do so. It would make sense that this person also be one of the presbyters if not the *episcopos*. If they could read, it also meant that they could lead the community in the reading and explication of scripture that was an important part of their weekly prayer services. The usual person to train those interested in becoming Christians, as well as to lead the initiation rites by which they were welcomed into the community, would be the presbyter or the *episcopos* who led the community. This meant that the leader of the community would have a central liturgical role.

The *episcopos* and *presbyteros* also had the important job of directing the charitable activities of the community. Under this leadership, the deacons visited the sick and those imprisoned, distributed food, and provided for the poor and destitute of the community. This act of providing charity was central to Christianity and was its most distinguishing characteristic. According to the great historian of early Christianity, Henry Chadwick, "the practical application of charity was probably the most potent single cause of Christian success."[2] This meant that, over time, the *episcopos* literally became a supervisor of what could be a large enterprise. Again according to Professor Chadwick, "By the year 251, the resources of the church in Rome had grown so much that it was supporting from its common purse not only the bishop, 46 presbyters, 7 deacons, 7 subdeacons, 42 acolytes, and 52 exorcists, readers and doorkeepers, but also more than 1500 widows and needy persons, all of whom were 'fed by the grace and kindness of the Lord.' "[3]

By the third century, a general pattern emerged, with some variations, in which Christian communities would have one *episcopos*, now more similar to a modern bishop, several presbyters, and several deacons. In large communities like Rome, a host of other lesser ministers would also help with either liturgical or charitable activities. Christianity was growing, and, inexorably, so was the organization needed to accomplish the aims of the Christian community: to continue to spread the message of Jesus, to celebrate the presence

2. Henry Chadwick, *The Early Church*, rev. ed. (New York: Penguin, 1993), 56.
3. Chadwick, *The Early Church*, 57–58.

of the risen Christ in worship, to continue to teach the community itself, and to organize the charitable activities that were the hallmark of the movement.

No Priests

One post that the early Christian community did not have was priest or priestess. The word for these jobs in Greek is *hiereus* and in Latin *sacerdos*. These were people who gave animal, grain, or wine offerings to a god or gods. It took the form of worship described in chapter 5 where an animal was slain (or other food offering was made to the gods), and then a meal ensued. Christians simply didn't need priests since they didn't have sacrifices. They had a meal, but that meal celebrated the one sacrifice of Jesus. This sacrifice never needed to be repeated, so they didn't need anyone to do the job. The only person called a "priest" in the early centuries of Christianity was the risen Christ. It just didn't make sense to call anyone else priest since no one else was performing a ritual sacrifice. By the third century, Christian leaders did start to use the term "priest" (*hiereus, sacerdos*) to refer to the person who led the Christian worship service, but only in the metaphoric sense that this person was celebrating the once and for all sacrifice of Jesus and that this celebration was a "sacrifice of praise." Once pagan priests and sacrifices slowly faded from the scene in those areas dominated by Christianity in the fifth and sixth centuries, the word priest changed its meaning and, somewhat ironically, came to become a common term for Christian ministers.

Beginnings of Monasticism

The fourth century brought two momentous changes to Christian ministry. The first of these changes affected all of Christianity, the latter mainly only those areas under control of the Roman Empire. Although its roots go back earlier, particularly in Syria, the fourth century saw the rise of a particular kind of vocation to the Christian life. For many reasons, some social and some religious, men and women wishing to live a more austere form of Christianity undertook a special form of discipline (or *askesis* in Greek). Based partly on medical knowledge of the time and partly on the social customs, these people removed themselves from society at large by not marrying and by retreating into some form of semi-reclusion. Men could leave for the desert of Egypt, the mountains of Syria, or even the top of a tall pole to practice prayer, fasting, and the development of "one heart": the ability to let the risen Christ shine through one's whole being and direct one's whole life. Women could do the same thing by retreating into an enclave within the family house. Those women who had been married but took on this new form of life after the death of their husbands were called "widows," a technical term referring to this new status in the community. Women who vowed never to marry became technically "virgins." Widows and virgins were highly esteemed by the community and were afforded a special place in the community liturgies.

These ascetics (one who undertook the discipline or practice) were seen as specially called by God and therefore, some argued, were holier than other Christians. These claims were disputed by "normal" married Christians, but a sometimes not so subtle pressure from the fourth century on was placed particularly on Christian ministers to take on the characteristics of the ascetics. Particularly, this meant not marrying. Some bishops, like the fourth-century bishop of Hippo, Augustine, encouraged their presbyters not to marry and to live in communities as some ascetics were doing. Although ministers would continue to marry in the Christian West until the twelfth century, and still do in Eastern Christianity, a gradual merging of two quite different vocations began. Ministers were gradually expected to live more and more like ascetics. In Eastern Christianity, bishops can only come from the ranks of those presbyters who are not married, and most often are ascetics (monks). In Western Christianity, marriage was forbidden to ministers in the early twelfth century, a custom that is continued among Roman Catholics to this day.

Constantine's Influence

A second momentous change took place when Christianity was adopted by the Emperor Constantine as his favored religion. Suddenly a religion which had just undergone one of the most severe of the sporadic persecutions unleashed on it by the government found itself part of that same government. Constantine lavished money on his new religion, building huge structures to house the Christian worship services. In the course of the fourth century, Christian ministers became paid officials of the Roman Empire. Bishops could hear certain kinds of law cases and were even allowed to wear the clothes assigned to the highest Roman officials. Actually, this was such a big deal that Christian ministers in some communities still wear these fancy Roman clothes when they celebrate the liturgy. Now existing in a very modified form and symbolizing a distant past, they are called "vestments." Few people remember where and why Christians started wearing them in the first place.

Christianity in the Roman Empire began to organize itself along the lines of the Roman government. The Roman government was organized into cities with their accompanying rural districts, cities were organized into provinces, and provinces were organized into the four large dioceses that made up the empire. By the fifth century, the church divisions were virtually coextensive with those of the empire. A bishop ruled a diocese (the same word, but used differently from the diocese of the empire), which corresponded to a Roman city; a metropolitan who was the bishop of the largest city in an area had responsibility for an area corresponding to the Roman province. In the major cities of Rome, Alexandria, Antioch, and Constantinople, the bishops took the title of patriarch and were responsible for the provinces in their regions. The patriarchates were the rough equivalent of the empire's dioceses. The Christians added a fifth patriarch to the four of the Roman government. The bishop of Jerusalem was also considered a patriarch as he was bishop of the founding city of Christianity. The patriarchs were also affectionately called "dad" by their congregations, or in Latin, *papa*, which in English became pope. The term now is used almost exclusively for the patriarch of Rome but was once used by all the patriarchs.

There were differences, of course. The church had no emperor over the patriarchs, each of which jealously guarded their own traditions and independence. Bishops, too, were comparatively independent, chosen by their own communities and almost always members of that community. The Council of Nicea declared that "neither bishop, presbyter, nor deacon shall pass from city to city. And if any one, after this decree of the holy and great Synod, shall attempt any such thing, or continue in any such course, his proceedings shall be utterly void, and he shall be restored to the Church for which he was ordained bishop or presbyter."[4] This decree was not always honored, alas, and political translations of bishops from one see to another did occur, but, in general, communities chose their own leaders from among their own people and greatly resented any interference by the Roman government. When George was installed by the government as patriarch of Alexandria, he lasted only as long as he was protected by Roman soldiers. When his escort disappeared due to a change of regime, a contemporary tells us, "the populace, transported with unexpected joy, gnashed their teeth, and with horrid outcries set upon George, trampling upon him and kicking him: they maltreated him in various ways, dragged him about spread-eagle fashion, and killed him."[5] Now George's mur-

---

4. Canon 15 of the Council of Nicea. The translation of the canons of Nicea quoted here is that of Henry R. Percival from *A Select Library of the Nicene and Post-Nicene Fathers of the Christian Church.* Paul Halsall has conveniently provided this translation online at the Web address http://www.fordham.edu/halsall/basis/nicea1 .txt.

5. The death of George is related by Ammianus Marcellinus, the fourth century historian, in his Res

derers were not (mainly) Christian, but the chronicler added that it would not have happened if the Christians had protected George, but they really hated his intrusion. The right of a community to appoint its own leaders continued for centuries in almost all Christian communities and continues today, with the odd exception of the Roman Catholics, an anomaly with which we will deal later.

Now in very large Christian communities outside the Roman Empire, particularly Christian communities under the rule of the Persian Empire, Christianity never became a state church. It remains under the control of a regime which was for centuries officially Zoroasterian and then later Moslem. These communities maintained their independence of the government, suffering occasional persecution but developing a learned theological and scholarly tradition upon which early Moslem rulers greatly depended. Aside from the large Persian Christian communities, other Christian communities outside the Roman Empire, including the Ethiopian, Armenian, and Thomas Christians of India maintain their independent organization to the present day. These churches were equally influenced, however, by the tendency to blend the vocations of asceticism and ministry to the community and have often chosen ascetics as their bishops and patriarchs.

Gradually a custom evolved, agreed to by nearly all of the Christian communities, whether or not they were under the Roman Empire, whereby the leaders of the diverse communities would gather together to settle the major issues facing Christianity in a great international or ecumenical council. Called sporadically to deal with specific issues, and more or less well attended, the decisions reached at these councils are still considered binding for the majority of Christians. By the end of the fifth century, then, a structure had emerged which saw the bishops as relatively independent Christian leaders under the regional leadership of patriarchs. When these leaders had serious disagreements, they would meet in council to decide jointly, and as nearly unanimously as possible, the important issues in Christian life and thought.

"Orders" and "Ordination" within the Church

All of the Christian churches were subject to another phenomenon of the ancient world. Most of that world was closely organized into different societal

---

Gestae. The passage quoted here is from the translation in J. Stevenson, ed., *Creeds, Councils and Controversies* (SPCK: London, 1973), 60–61.

states, vocations, professions, or jobs. The word for a state, vocation, profession, or job was in Latin an *ordo*. Marriage was an *ordo*; to be a carpenter was an *ordo*; the senators belonged to a unique *ordo*; the emperor was in his own *ordo*. These *ordines* (the plural for *ordo*) were tightly regulated. Each *ordo* had its own legal standing, commonly its own part of the city in which to live, and even its own distinctive clothes. In fact, it was the change in *ordo* that allows Christian ministers to wear the high-class Roman clothes that mutated into liturgical vestments.

Frequently there were initiation ceremonies involved when a person entered a new *ordo*. Such a ceremony was called an *ordinatio* in Latin, and this is where we get the English word "ordination." Christians, just like any other group of the time, had its *ordines*. Bishops, presbyters, deacons, deaconesses, monks, widows, virgins—all were *ordines* in the church. So were the lesser offices of church doormen (porters), candle-holders (acolytes), exorcists, and readers (lectors). Any job within the Christian community was an *ordo*, and there were any number of *ordinationes* (the plural of *ordinatio*) that were celebrated when one moved to a new ministry in the Christian community.

Not all the ministries were equally important or influential, of course, so some *ordinationes* were a bigger deal than others, but they were all ordinations. This was the very same word, *ordinatio*, that would be used for the anointing of the emperor or the appointment of a mayor. All these were *ordinationes*. Christians were simply following the societal customs of the time by celebrating the appointment of a member of their community to a new ministry within that community. Everybody had *ordinationes*; so did Christians.

Early Christian Ordinations

The ordination of a bishop was the most elaborate of these ceremonies. First, the bishop had to be chosen by the community, particularly by the other ministers in the community, but with the approval of the entire community. The newly chosen bishop was then approved by the bishops in the surrounding area by their laying hands on him. This way, the choice of the people was ratified, accepted, and approved by the universal church as symbolized by the bishops of the area. This universal connection of a local church to the larger Christianity is often referred to as "catholicity," since *catholicos* is the Greek word for universal. This laying on of hands was an important "seal of approval," demonstrating that the particular community in question and its newly chosen leader were acceptable to the larger "catholic/universal" Christian community.

The laying on of hands, however, which could take place at the regular weekly Christian prayer service was surely the most dramatic moment in the process but did not in itself constitute an ordination. The fourth-century Roman Pope Leo the Great held that a valid ordination of a bishop could not occur unless the bishop had been chosen by the clergy, accepted by the Christian community, and consecrated by the bishops of the province along with the ranking bishop of the area.

Presbyters were ordained by their bishops, as were deacons and the other lesser ministries of the church. Again the ceremony would most often take place during the weekly prayer service with the bishop laying hands on those to be ordained. Sometimes those being ordained were also presented with a sign of their ministry. A book, for instance, would be presented to a lector.

The ceremonies were fairly simple, and the essentials of the ceremony have remained the same over centuries. The laying on hands and the presentation of a sign of the ministry in question take place in the presence of the community to be served, often in the context of the usual Christian prayer service. The understanding of ministry and of the authority that goes with it, however, has changed much over the centuries. Sadly, the different understandings of ministry and authority in the Christian community are also the biggest obstacles to Christian unity, and so deserve some explanation.

"Normative" Periods in Church History

Many Christian groups look to the period of the fourth and fifth centuries as a golden era in Christian history. This period is "normative" for those groups in the sense that the theology and (most important) the church structure that emerged in this period set the "norm" or the standard for present practice. The present Eastern Orthodox communion of churches descends directly from the churches of this period and include the traditional patriarchates of Constantinople, Alexandria, Antioch, and Jerusalem, as well as the more recent patriarchates of Russia, Serbia, Romania, Bulgaria, and Georgia and the Orthodox churches of Cyprus, Greece, the Czech Republic and Slovakia, Poland, and Albania. These communities continue the structure described above in the governing of their communities with amazingly little change.

They are not the only churches, however, that look to this period and the structures adopted by the Christianity of the time. So, too, do the ancient communities represented by the Assyrian Church, the Coptic Church, the Ethiopian Church, the Armenian Church, the Syrian Orthodox Church, and the Mar Thomas Syrian Church of India, although they are not necessarily in communion with the patriarchates mentioned above or even with each other. Prob-

ably one of the largest collections of Christian churches that look to the structures of the fifth century as the model for church government are the
Episcopalian churches, which consist of the Anglican Communion of national
churches and other churches in communion with this grouping, including the
Episcopal Church of the United States of America (commonly called "Episcopalians").

All these groups, which include some of the most ancient Christian communities, are governed by relatively independent bishops under whom serve
priests and deacons. Most have patriarchs as well, or at least an archbishop
(bishop over bishops) to which the bishops would look for guidance and leadership. The patriarchs are understood as equals, independently representing
their churches, although most would agree that the ancient patriarchates have
some at least honorary precedence. All would look to councils as the definitive
decision-making bodies of Christianity where the bishops meet to represent
their communities in discussions affecting all of Christianity.

The Split between Eastern and Western Christianity

As the judicious reader will quickly note, most of the churches mentioned
above, with the notable exception of the Anglican/Episcopalian churches, are
the churches established on the eastern banks of the Mediterranean Sea along
with their daughter churches. On the northern and western banks of the Mediterranean, other church structures emerged. One of the major reasons for
these developments was simple enough. Unlike the eastern Mediterranean,
the West had only one patriarchate, that of the bishop of Rome. Already by the
end of the fifth century, the eastern and western Mediterranean groups began
to very slowly drift apart, separated by the invasion of the Germanic tribes who
eventually conquered and ruled in the West, displacing the Roman Empire.
Meanwhile in the East the two great empires of Rome and Persia continued
to reign, and the lesser Christian kingdoms of Ethiopia and Armenia retained
at least nominal independence.

The church in the West became, in many respects, the only functioning
part of the Roman government left in that region. The patriarchs of Rome,
especially the two popes called "Great," Leo I and Gregory I, organized the
local government, negotiated peace with the Germanic and Asiatic warlords,
and financed missionary efforts among the newly dominant tribes. Cut off
from the East, the popes of Rome came more and more adamantly to assert
earlier Roman claims that the other patriarchs were subject to Rome.

At this point, the Roman government was intrinsically linked to the Christian churches under its reign. The emperor claimed to hold a sacred *ordo* as much as any patriarch, bishop, or priest. Conflicts over the relative authority of the different *ordines* of patriarch or bishop and emperor could become fierce and dangerous, even violent. When the emperor moved the capital of the empire to Constantinople in the fourth century, the patriarch of Rome became the most independent of the patriarchates simply because it was the most distant from the new capital. Of course, as Rome became more and more isolated from the eastern Empire and its seat of power in Constantinople, the patriarch of Rome became even more independent of the empire.

By the eighth century, the Roman patriarchate felt secure enough in its own authority to anoint the most successful of the Germanic warlords, the Frankish leader Charles the Great (Charlemagne) as emperor of the entire Roman Empire. This bold act embodied the growing claims by the patriarchs of Rome that they were the head of the entire universal (catholic) Christian community. Both the emperor and the other patriarchs were subject to the authority of Rome. Needless to say, neither the emperor in Constantinople (or actually at the time of Charlemagne, the Empress Irene) nor the other patriarchs were inclined to accept these claims. By the eighth century, however, there was little they could do about it. The patriarchates of Alexandria, Antioch, and Jerusalem, while still vibrant, were now under control of the newly assurgent Islam, and Constantinople was occupied with holding the Islamic armies at bay.

To relate the entire sad story of the gradual drift apart of the patriarchate of Rome from the other patriarchs would take up too much space, but at least by the eleventh century when the patriarchs of Rome and Constantinople exchanged mutual excommunications, it was becoming clear that a different form of church governance was evolving in Western Christianity, one which claimed that the pope, the patriarch of Rome, was the head of the entire Christian community worldwide; further, it was clear that the other patriarchs were not going to accept that claim. Although there are other serious disagreements between the eastern churches and Rome, as well as between the churches of the Anglican/Episcopal communion and Rome, few would dispute that central to their present mutual lack of recognition is the claim of Rome to be the unique leader of Christianity.

Roman Leadership in the Middle Ages

The claims of the Roman popes to be head of the universal Christian community did not go unchallenged even in Western Christianity. In fact, throughout much of what is commonly called the "Middle Ages" in European history, the papacy and secular governments struggled for control over the Christian communities in the West. In the eleventh and twelfth centuries, the papacy made an exerted effort to remove control of Christian communities from lay control of the lords. These efforts met with some success, and the form of Western Christianity that emerged would continue to influence Western Christianity and those Christian communities formed by missionary movements from the West until the present.

The governing structures of the Western church of the thirteenth through sixteenth centuries had several distinctive characteristics. First, true sacramental *ordinatio* was limited to only three offices: that of priest, deacon, and subdeacon. All other rites of installation to new ministries in the Christianity community were now no longer considered "real" ordinations. Further, only men could aspire to these three ministries. Women could no longer be "ordained," and all other former *ordines*, including those of abbot, abbess, monk, nun, lector, king, and queen, were now considered "simple layfolk." The gap between "clergy" and "laity" widened and deepened. Only the clergy could now hear confessions, lead the weekly prayer service, even read the gospel aloud at services. Theologians began to speculate that those truly ordained were somehow metaphysically different from all the other members of the Christian community.

Most strikingly, as least for most modern readers, was the insistence that those ordainedwould not be able to contract a valid marriage. Of course, there was already a longstanding tendency to urge Christian ministers to become ascetics, which included the renunciation of an active sex life. These reforms went further, however, and ruled that once ordained, a priest, deacon, or subdeacon could not contract a valid marriage at all. Since Christian morality forbids sexuality outside one's own marriage, this effectively forced all (moral) ministers to become ascetics. Like ascetics, ministers were also required to read special prayers several times a day (called "the office"). The reformers knew that ministers in other Christian communities married and that Christian ministers in their own communities had been legally married for centuries, so this new law was considered a merely human law introduced for good order in the community. The idea was that since ascetics were holier than ordinary Christians, then making all ministers ascetics would make for holier ministers. This rule also went a long way to remove clergy from the dynastic intrigues of medieval government and protected church lands from loss through inheritance. Whether this reform actually accomplished these goals is hotly disputed to this day. The change was an important one, however, as the

Roman Catholic Church has continued to enforce this law down to the present day.

The Rise of the Papacy

Another important change was the role of the papacy as a sort of "court of last appeal" within the Christian community. Bishops still retained a great deal of their independence, and they were still chosen by the local clergy with the approval of the laity, but in certain issues, a dispute could be appealed over the head of the bishop to Rome. Since marriage was one of the areas over which church courts had control, ordinary people were often affected. If they could not get justice from their local lord, they could appeal to the bishop. If they could not get justice from the local bishop (who could very likely be a relative of the lord), they could appeal to Rome. For many people this was very liberating and very exciting. Take, for instance, the case of a young woman who was forced to marry a husband chosen by her parents, which was the usual means of obtaining a spouse up until this period. The young lady in question could sneak off to the bishop and claim she had never consented to the marriage, and the marriage would be annulled. The parents could kick and scream all they wanted, but consent of the two parties marrying constituted a marriage, and the bishop (or the pope if the bishop was in on the arranged marriage) could and did defend this position.

By now the reader has probably seen the downside to this approach to Christian ministry. It can and was used to defend the rights of the helpless against some fairly ruthless lords, but it also created a vast legal system. More and more, service to the Christian community became service in a legalistic bureaucracy which threatened to burgeon out of control. Bishops became more like medieval lords than servants to their people, and the pope became more like an emperor; in fact, the pope claimed the right to appoint the emperor. Now this kind of legal and political power can be used for good (and often enough was), but it can also corrupt (and sadly enough did).

Already by the beginning of the fourteenth century, prophetic voices in the community were calling for reform. By the beginning of the fifteenth century, the voices had become a chorus and since reform was not seen as likely to come from Rome, a movement began to reform the Christian community without the support or consent of Rome.

Before moving on to the great sixteenth-century reform movement, it is worth pointing out that the medieval West produced a quite different form of

Christian ministry than that of the fifth century. Here the bishops, still largely independent and chosen by their communities, looked to Rome for a centralized form of legal governance. Rome could intervene in a disputed election of a bishop, for instance. Rome acted as an appellate court in marriage and other cases. Rome claimed to legislate for the entire universal Christian community, even though, in fact, her decrees had little or no effect outside of western Europe. Ministers were expected to act more like ascetics and were clearly separate from the laity over whom they ruled. Women could definitely not share in this governance. Only ordained ministers could effectively perform most of the Christian rituals, and so they were of the utmost importance in the lives of everyday Christians. Under ordinary circumstances, a Christian could not be baptized, married, or buried, and could not even celebrate a regular Christian prayer service, without a priest.

This form of Christian ministry is of interest because, although with some important modifications noted below, this is the model of Christian ministry used by the Roman Catholic Church, by far the largest Christian community in the world. It has all the advantages of a centralized, international organization. Aid can be rushed anywhere in the world quickly and effectively. Thousands of local communities can be mobilized for political or social action in no time at all. A single spokesperson, the pope, can speak out forcefully on issues of social justice. The problems of a legalistic bureaucracy also remain, however, and Roman Catholicism has to be constantly on guard against a clericalism and legalism that can get in the way of Christian charity and service. So here we have a second model of Christian ministry which looks to the thirteenth century, rather than the fifth century, as the normative period for Christian service.

The Reformations of the Sixteenth Century

In the sixteenth century, Christianity in western Europe split into several mutually antagonistic groups, each of which significantly changed the Christianity that had been practiced in the late Middle Ages. In this particular section, however, only those changes that affected the structure of Christian ministry are discussed.

Usually considered the earliest and most influential of the Reformers, the German Augustinian priest and theologian, Martin Luther (1483–1546) challenged the stark differentiation between clergy and laity in the late medieval church, arguing that the ministry belonged to all the members of the church: "There is neither cleric nor layman, nor status of this or that order, not he who prays nor he who reads, but to all these things a man is indifferent, doing or not doing them as shall help or take away from charity" (Commentary on Galatians).[6] Luther did not mean by this to abolish all distinctions between ministers and congregations, but he did intend that the difference would be based on function rather than status. The difference between clergy and laity, therefore, was that clergy were officially called and ordained to particular jobs or ministries in the church, ministries which no one could take on themselves without ecclesiastical approval. But such approval did not give clergy any special status. Luther particularly opposed the ascetic life as having any special status in the Christian community. Thus he allowed and even encouraged the clergy to marry, himself marrying an ex-nun. Luther also claimed that the laity had the duty to organize and protect the church and called on the government leaders in Germany to support, defend, and implement the reforms needed in the church. The Reformed movement certainly saw no need for any sort of separation of church and state. On the contrary, the state's role was to protect, defend, and enforce church teaching. To this day, Lutheran ministers in Germany, Sweden, Denmark, and Norway, for instance, are paid by the government.

John Calvin (1509–1564), the influential preacher of reform in Geneva, unlike Luther, did understand the clergy as having a separate status from laity. Based on a close reading of scripture, Calvin understood four ministries to have been established by scripture: pastor, teacher, elder, and deacon. The pastor proclaimed the word of God, the teacher's role was to study the word of God, the elders were to enforce discipline in the church, and the deacons were to care for the poor. Like Luther, however, Calvin felt it was the duty of the civil government to enforce the decrees of the church, even to the point of exiling or executing those guilty in the eyes of the church.

Important to both Luther and Calvin was that ministers are "called" by their communities. Although this might be done in different ways in different communities, each minister is appointed by a particular community for ministry in that community. Based on this understanding, most Lutheran and Calvinist ministers are "called" (essentially hired and fired) by their respective communities.

Both Luther and Calvin retained forms of ordination, ceremonies whereby ministers are judged by the competent authorities to be orthodox and capable of ministry. Present Reformed liturgies consist roughly of the following procedure. First, the candidates are examined on their orthodoxy, their morality,

6. Quoted in Bernard Reardon, *Religious Thought in the Reformation*, 2nd ed. (London: Longman, 1995), 69.

and the authenticity of their vocation. If found worthy, they are formally accepted by the community. Then the congregation prays for the candidates, and finally, usually as part of a regular Sunday service, the candidates are ordained either by the laying on of hands by the presiding minister or ministers, or by the prayers of the people and ministers. In some congregations, the newly ordained are then offered the right hand of fellowship by their fellow ministers.

Roman Catholic Practice

Those Western Christians who continued to see the pope as the head of all of Christianity are now most commonly known as Roman Catholic, although the designation had been used earlier for Western Christians in general. Like those who inaugurated reforms unacceptable to the pope, primarily the followers of Luther and Calvin as well as the church in England, the Roman Catholics also reformed the practices of the late Middle Ages.

They continued to see priests as having a separate and higher status than the laity and considered ordination as a ceremony that set the clergy apart from as well as above their congregations. Following the lead of Luther and Calvin, however, a much higher standard of education was required of the clergy. Most important, the Roman Catholic Church refused to accept as valid any ordination which took place in the Reformed community. Subsequently, any ceremony (with the exception of baptism) performed by a Reformed minister was understood to be invalid. After centuries of discussion, it was decided that the same was true of the Anglican communion. This meant that Roman Catholics do not recognize as valid any Sunday service or any ordination performed by Reformed or Anglican clergy.

In the late nineteenth century another important and far-reaching change took place in Roman Catholic practice. Up until that time, Roman Catholic bishops were either chosen by their congregations or appointed by the local government; this was basically a continuation of earlier practice and consistent with the practice of Reformed congregations. The pope himself was (and continues to be) elected by a special group of ministers called "cardinals." However, at the very end of the nineteenth century, the pope claimed the right to appoint all Roman Catholic bishops throughout the world. This claim was embodied in the Code of Canon (church) Law that was approved by Pope Benedict XV in 1917. Since then, despite sometimes fierce opposition by local communities, the pope has appointed all Roman Catholic bishops without the approval of their respective communities. Roman Catholic bishops also appoint priests to local churches with only a formality of local consent. This too has sometimes led in the past to strong opposition on the part of the local congregations. This change markedly distinguishes the ministry of the Roman Catholic Church from all other Christian churches.

Modern Developments

In the last hundred years, other changes have also occurred in the way Christians have chosen their ministers and carried out their ministry. Many Christian groups now once again ordain women as ministers and even bishops. The exceptions here are Eastern Orthodox and Roman Catholic churches who argue that women cannot be validly ordained Christian ministers.

Often based on clothes popular in the sixteenth or even nineteenth centuries, ministers in several Christian congregations up until the middle of the twentieth century wore distinctive garb. Most ministers are now indistinguishable from their secular counterparts. This can be taken as one sign that distinction between clergy and laity is beginning to disappear.

The trend toward democratization has also marked many Christian groups. Christian leaders are more and more commonly elected by a vote of the community or some representative body of that community. As well, change in practice or doctrine can be subjected to a vote by the community or its representatives. The exception again here is the Roman Catholic and Eastern Orthodox communities where (with the exception of the pope who is elected by the cardinals), Christian leaders and teaching are determined by the leadership of the church, not by vote.

Why All This History?

Astute readers will certainly wonder at this point why this chapter consists mostly of the history of how ministry developed in Christian history, particularly in Western Christianity. This may seem particularly odd, as the main purpose of Christian ministry is secondary to the central aim of Christians, which is to attain salvation as has been described in chapter 2. How ministry has fostered (or hindered) this process may seem pretty irrelevant.

History in this case is important for several reasons. First, the major splits between Christian groups often entail ministry and its authority within Christianity. Some Roman Catholics would argue, for instance, that salvation is difficult, if not impossible, without sacraments, and sacraments are not possible without properly ordained ministers. Most Reformed Christians would deny this, insisting that salvation depends entirely on the risen Christ. Further, since Roman Catholics do not recognize ministers ordained outside the Roman Catholic Church, salvation outside that church would be considered extraordinary even if it were possible for those outside Roman Catholicism. Should all Christians be under the authority of the pope? Or of bishops? Or are all congregations independent of one another? Such questions have been a major source of division among Christians. This division is a scandal, to be sure, but at least it is easier to understand if one knows the history behind the divisions.

Second, this history helps explain the diversity of ministries among the different Christian groups: why some are called "episcopalians," some "presbyterians," and some "congregationalists." Christians are often classified depending upon the way they have organized themselves. This is again an indication that the use of authority and power within the ministry has had a central role in dividing Christianity into separate groups.

Third, the history of Christian ministry makes clear how much that ministry is shaped by current political systems. Christian ministry tends to mirror whatever political structure happens to shape the secular society in which the church exists. When Christian groups do not mirror the present structures, it is usually because they are choosing some earlier secular structure as "normative" in the sense explained above. From a historical point of view, there does not seem to be any one pattern of ministry that is essentially Christian. Rather, Christians have borrowed structures of authority from Judaism, from the Roman Empire, from medieval feudalism, from the emerging nation-states of the sixteenth century, from divine-right monarchy, and now from representative democracy. It should not be surprising, therefore, that Christian ministry is constantly in a state of flux and that it will continue to evolve as the secular society around it changes.

Church members can find this disconcerting, since ministry can present itself as divinely established and therefore unchanging. When inevitable change does occur, people feel that they have been somehow cheated, that they have been misled, and their faith is shaken. If one remembers that the role of ministry is secondary to the central purpose of Christianity and Christians can choose whatever structures they feel will best serve salvation, some of this insecurity can be avoided and even the tension between Christian groups might be somewhat eased.

This is easier said than done, however. As explained in chapter 1, power always plays a part in the performance of human ritual. Consequently, at best, power has had an ambiguous role for the ministers whose central role is to perform those rituals. On the one hand, terrible atrocities have been committed by Christians through the misuse of power: the Crusades, the Inquisition, the witch hunts of the early modern period, ongoing anti-Semitism, and misogyny. On the other hand, great good has been done: the ending of legal infanticide, freedom from arranged marriage, the abolition of slavery, the support of work-ers' rights and of civil rights in general. Historians and individuals radically disagree whether Christianity has been a source for more good or more evil in the world, but that they do disagree at least highlights the role that the use and abuse of power has had in Christian ministry. One should hardly be surprised by this. As discussed above, humans seem inevitably to organize themselves, and this organization inevitably involves power, and power is very seductive. Many people, even Christians, succumb to the temptation. The history of min-istry tells us how Christians came to be divided as they are and warns Chris-tians about the dangers involved in the use of power and authority.

Christian Ministry

Christian ministry is fundamentally the attempt by Christians to get things done that are worth doing: proclaiming the word of God, performing Christian rituals, managing the finances, providing education for those interested in joining the community and for the young, as well as for the continuing edu-cation of the membership. Someone also has to have some means to decide who is living the Christian life and who is not. Scholars need to continue to recover the meaning of scripture and Christian tradition and help understand how best to live that message today. Ministers do all of the above and often much more.

This is a particularly challenging job because Christianity, for the reasons mentioned above, has often confused the vocation of ascetics with that of min-isters. Ministers are then expected to be "holier" than other Christians, and higher standards are expected of them. This places tremendous pressure on ministers (and their families) and has the added nefarious effect of letting "ordinary" Christians think that they are off the hook. If there are "profes-sional" Christians (the ministers) who do our "God-work" for us, we don't have to be all that Christian ourselves. It's their job to be good, even to pray us into heaven while we operate in the "real world" where we need to be nasty to survive.

Of course, all this is a parody and a travesty of what Christianity was meant to be. As Luther in particular emphasized in the sixteenth century, all Chris-tians are called to the same standards of life, whatever job they have to do in the community. No particular job is "holier" than another job. Those who don't marry aren't holier than those who do. Those who preach the word of God aren't holier than those who hear. Most Christians would immediately agree with the above statements, but Christians don't always live up to these beliefs. All of which means that Christian ministry will continue to be a challenge to both those who are called to formal ministry and those who are not. Christians must continually ask themselves how best to organize themselves to carry out the continuing work of the risen Christ while minimizing the temptations to misuse any power given to them to do that work.

Five Elements of Ritual

Hermeneutic of Experience

The central job of a minister is explaining, by word or example, how Christians interpret reality. Most obviously, preachers relate the word of God to the political, social, and economic realities of their communities, but other ministries also fulfill these functions. Deacons traditionally care for the poor, and this ministry is now carried by thousands of Christians throughout the world. Even when they do not have any official ordination ceremony, they are still the successors to the ancient deacons and, thus, model to all Christians how financial resources of Christians are to be rightly used. Ministers to the sick teach Christians to interpret the reality of illness and even death as opportunities to grow in the life of the risen Christ. Christian marriage counselors, again whether officially ordained or not, help others understand relationships as signs of God's love for humans. And so the list goes on. All ministry demonstrates by service that Christians are meant to serve others in the world as Jesus served those around him during his lifetime. Most important, Christian ministers are called to demonstrate in their lives how power can be used for service.

Maturation

Since ministry, even as service, often entails the use of power, ministers must be mature enough to use power without abusing it. Already in the New Testament, the requirements for leadership demanded maturity and the ability to handle authority:

> The president must have an impeccable character. He must not have
> been married more than once, and he must be temperate, discreet
> and courteous, hospitable and a good teacher; not a heavy drinker,
> not hot-tempered, but kind and peaceable. He must not be a lover of
> money. He must be a man who manages his own family well and

brings his children up to obey him and be well-behaved: how can a man who does not understand how to manage his own family have responsibility for the church of God? (1 Tim. 3:2–5)

Of course, for most Christian groups today, the text should read "she" as well as "he." The ideal Christian minister should be a person mature enough not to be seduced by wealth or power and model this maturity for other Christians.

Presence

Ministers make the risen Christ present to others in their ministry. When church groups take care of the sick, poor, and homeless, they are carrying on the work started by Jesus when he was alive, thus making him present to those to whom they minister. This living presence of the risen Christ, made visible in acts of caring, is celebrated in all the rituals over which ministers preside, but particularly in the Sunday service. Ministry is where the risen Christ most obviously "comes alive" to most people: when they are touched, helped, cured, aided, housed, or clothed by a Christian, most often one designated to perform this function by their local, national, or international community. It is the reading of the word and the sharing of the blessed bread and wine that celebrates this kind of life and empowers its members to continue to live it.

Service

Nothing is so central to ministry as service. The only purpose of ministry is service to the Christian community, which is itself, in turn, a community of service. Jesus made it abundantly clear that he wished to serve others and that those who followed him should do the same. In the gospel of John Jesus is portrayed as washing the feet of his followers, a job done by the lowliest of the servants. Jesus left no doubt as to the meaning of his actions: "I have given you an example so that you may copy what I have done to you" (John 13:15). Christians have not always lived up to this disconcerting challenge, but every Christian is called to serve others to the best of her or his ability. The different ministries within the church are simply the different forms of service necessary to keep the work of Jesus alive.

Friendship

In the farewell discourse from the Gospel of John, Jesus informed his followers that "I give you a new commandment: love one another; just as I have loved you, you must love one another. By this love you have for one another, everyone will know that you are my disciples" (John 13:34–35) and again in the same passage: "You are my friends, if you do what I command you. I shall not call you servants any more, because a servant does not know his master's business; I call you friends, because I have made known to you everything I have learned from the Father" (John 14:14–15). Jesus intended his followers to be friends in service to friends, a service based on love. It would be a tough act to follow; Jesus had high standards for friendship: "A person can have no greater love than to lay down his life for his or her friends" (John 14:13). If ministry is service, it is also friendship. Christian ministers should serve out of friendship and certainly not use their authority to bully or berate or belittle others. Condescension has no place in Christian service. Ministers are not lords, masters, or even corporate executives. They should be friends helping other friends to make it easier for them, in turn, to help others. Again, the temptation to misuse power and authority are very strong here, but Jesus has already given Christians a model of how to do this and the risen Christ empowers them to be able to do it.

In conclusion, service is at the heart of Christianity, and all Christians are called to service. Some particular functions in Christianity are marked out by special ceremonies, *ordinationes* in Latin, to celebrate the entrance of that person into a new form of service to the community. Down through history, Christians have exercised these ministries in many different ways, although usually in ways that mirror the social forms of authority around them. In each of these differing structures of service and authority, the temptation exists to abuse one's position to amass power or wealth, or both. Yet, the proper use of power and authority can and has done great good in the world. Most likely Christians will continue to form structures of service based on the political structures around them; most likely they will continue to struggle with the temptations of wealth and power. Certainly, however, they will constantly strive to build structures and ministries that make possible the central mission of Christianity, which is to continue the work of the risen Christ to serve and heal all those in need.

8

Rituals for Healing, Suffering, Death

Humans have always needed and still need healing—healing from sickness and physical debility, healing from psychological illness, healing from dysfunctional societies and oppression, healing from sin. This has meant that God's action of salvation has always been one of healing: of working against the evils that afflict humans and diminish the quality of their lives and in many cases threaten their very survival. To put it another way, a central feature of human life has always been the reality of suffering and the threat of death and the accompanying need of help from God.

Ancient literature and the earliest historical accounts are filled with stories of humans trying to face the evil forces in human experience and the many attempts to obtain some "divine" help in this struggle. To take but one example, the Hebrew Bible is a witness to the constant seeking of divine help in the struggle of the people of Israel to survive and prosper, despite the attacks of enemies like Egypt and Assyria: to overcome floods and famine and the disastrous results of their own misguided and sinful behavior. Like other peoples, the Israelites try to obtain the favor of God through celebration of rituals, eventually focusing on the ritual offerings of the temple in Jerusalem.

At the time of Jesus, it was the rituals of the temple that Jews believed was their means of gaining from their God Yahweh the help and protection and healing that they needed. Jesus himself as he was growing into maturity shared in the liturgies of the temple, prayed along with other pilgrims the temple Psalms that pleaded with God for healing, forgiveness, and protection. As he began his prophetic mission, however, he introduced into the picture his own power of healing and his own forgiveness of sin. He claimed to be empowered by the Spirit of God and proved this by his miracles of healing.

What is interesting and very significant is that Jesus' healings were always performed in the context of people's faith. It was as if the special power he possessed touched the faith of those who needed healing and so they were healed. Often, as the healing occurred, Jesus ended by saying to the person, "Go, now, your faith has made you whole." Jesus' healings were "faith healings" in the deepest sense of that term, and the gospels record that he was unable to perform such healing in situations where people did not have true faith but only fascination with spectacular happenings.

Perhaps it was to avoid any implication of magic that Jesus ordinarily used no complicated external gestures in his healings; he simply said, "Be healed," "Take up your bed and walk," or he touched the person. On at least one occasion, however, he did use a more detailed action—a ritual, though not what people would have considered "a religious ritual." It was the time when a blind man approached him asking for the gift of sight. Jesus in reply reached down, made a mud cake from the dust, applied it to the eyes of the man, and then told him to wash in a nearby pool. It may be that the gospel recalls and records this ritualized healing because it was repeated in some early Christian practice, for we do know that the earliest Christians used rituals like baptizing to bring about the inner healing of humans from evil. Like Jesus himself, Christians were careful that the elements of ritual did not come to be seen as magically effective. Rather, the external features of the ritual, especially whatever words were used, pointed to the inner intent of healing that carried the power of God's creative Spirit.

Obviously, there are many areas of needed healing—physical, psychological, and social—and it was precisely to this healing that Jesus' public mission was directed. When the gospels summarize Jesus' prophetic activity they say that "Jesus taught and Jesus healed." But not only Jesus himself was empowered by God's Spirit to work against person-diminishing forces; Jesus passed on that empowerment to his disciples. As one examines the kind of power that Jesus gave to Peter, then to the Twelve, then to all his disciples, it is clear that it was the power to overcome evil, all evil but especially the evil of sin. It is the use of this power that Christian rituals are meant to exercise.

Healing in Christian History

Christians have always taken very seriously their obligation to heal the world around them. In fact, the reaching out of the Christian community to those in need distinguished them from most other groups in the ancient world. The exception would be the Jewish community, who were well known for their care of the less well off in their community. Christians, however, reached out to all in need, Christian or not. By the year 251, the Church of Rome was supporting more than 1,500 people in need. According to the famous historian of early Christianity, Henry Chadwick:

> The practical application of charity was probably the most potent single cause of Christian success. The pagan comment, "See how these Christians love one another" (reported by Tertullian) was not irony. Christian charity expressed itself in care for the poor, for widows and orphans, in visits to brethren in prison or condemned to the living death of labour in the mines, and in social action in time of calamity like famine, earthquake, pestilence, or war.[1]

As Christians grew in number and wealth, their outreach also increased. In the fourth century, two Christians, Fabiola of Rome and Basil of Caesaria, established large centers of care, the beginnings of the modern hospital. These centers did more than care for the sick, however. As well as caring for the sick, they provided a home for the elderly whose families could not care for them, they provided hostels for travelers, and they took in families out of work and trained them in new vocations. Basil's care center was so large that the local Roman officials became worried. Basil responded, describing the work done there:

> And whom do we wrong when we build hospices for strangers, for those who visit us while on a journey, for those who require some care because of sickness, and when we extend to the latter the necessary comforts such as nurses, physicians, beasts for traveling, and attendants? There must also be occupations to go with these men, both those that are necessary for gaining a livelihood, and also such as have been discovered for a civilized mode of live. (Letter to Elias, Governor of Cappadocia)[2]

---

1. Henry Chadwick, *The Early Church*, rev. ed. (London: Penguin Books, 1993), 56.
2. The passage quoted here is from the translation in Stevenson, *Creeds, Councils and Controversies*, 105.

Christians embarked on social welfare on a grand scale in their efforts to heal not only individual but societal illnesses. When 7,000 Persian soldiers were taken captive by the Romans in 422, Bishop Acacius of Amida (in Turkey) melted down all the cups and plates used in the church. He used the proceeds not only to free the Persians but also to purchase all the supplies they would need to return home to Persia. At the time, the majority of Persians were not only non-Christian but were the bitter enemies of the Romans.[3]

Not all Christians, alas, have lived up to the wonderful examples of Fabiola of Rome, Basil of Caesaria, and Acacius of Amida. However, many have, and the Christian tradition of care and healing has extended down through the centuries and up to the present moment. Some religious orders and organizations are specifically dedicated to helping those in need, such as the medieval Hospitallers who swore "to treat the poor as Lords," the modern Salvation Army, and the Missionaries of Charity founded by Mother Teresa of Calcutta.

Christians from the beginning and without pause during Christianity's 2,000-year history have understood practical healing of individuals and societies as central to their way of life. As one would imagine, this practical approach was combined with prayer and ritual. In fact, throughout most of Christian history, prayer and ritual would have been understand as themselves practical applications of charity. Most Christians in the past and many Christians today would see prayer itself as having the power of healing social, psychological, and even physical illnesses. A few groups, like the Church of Christ, Scientist (Christian Science), founded by Mary Baker Eddy (1821–1910), hold that illness is an illusion that can be healed only by awareness of God's power and love rather than by medical treatment. The majority of Christians, however, hold that prayer is one important part of a larger attempt to cure the many ills that afflict the human race.

History of Rituals of Healing

The first description of Christian healing ritual is contained in the Letter of James: "Is any among you sick? Let him call for the elders of the church, and let them pray over this person, anointing the person with oil in the name of the Lord; and the prayer of faith will save the sick person and the Lord will

---

3. The account of the generosity of Acacius is related in the history of the church written in the fifth century by Socrates. The passage quoted here is from the translation in Stevenson, *Creeds, Councils and Controversies*, 258–59.

raise that person up; and if the person has committed sins, the person will be forgiven" (James 5:14–15).

The practice seems to have changed little over the centuries. A sick person would be anointed with oil, and prayers would be said for his or her recovery. One imagines that much of this was quite informal. The local community would pray for those who were ill among them, and sometimes a church leader would be called to anoint the ill person. Over time, the ritual of anointing was delayed until the point of death, particularly in the Latin West. This ritual was known as "the last anointing" or "extreme unction." From the twelfth to the fifteenth century, and for Roman Catholics until the twentieth century, ritual anointing of the sick was done only for those on the verge of death.

Less formal rituals, however, certainly continued. The ill were mentioned in prayer as a regular part of the Sunday liturgy. People would seek out particularly holy people (living or dead) or places where healing took place and offer special prayers. One form of petition, common in some communities until the present day, is to place a small picture or image of the injured area of the body (called an "ex voto") near a statue or tomb of a saint in hopes that that saint would intervene with God on behalf of the sick person. Another common practice was (and is) to offer a certain set number of days of prayer (called a "novena" since nine is a common number of days in this practice) in hopes for the recovery of an ill person. Another practice used to ask for God's protection for greater social or natural evils such as war or famine is the procession. Under the leadership of the clergy, people would march (or "process") through the community with a sacred symbol (a statue or consecrated host) while in prayer petitioning God to avert the evil in question.

More Recent Practices

The Reformers of the sixteenth century generally did away with the practice of anointing the dying. They did continue the practice of praying for and over ill persons. Particularly in the Pentecostal tradition, prayers over the sick and hurting are common parts of the worship service. Dramatic and intense, these healing services involve the ill person coming forward and often the hands of the minister are placed on the person while the community prays for healing. Unfortunately, these rituals have sometimes been ridiculed in the popular media because of a few high-profile charlatans who fake cures during such ceremonies. These few aberrations should not detract from the Pentecostal tradition's powerful use of prayer, almost always accompanied by care for the sick.

This form of Christianity has most clearly retained the mixture of prayer and care that marked the early Christian communities.

For some decades now those Christians who continue an official ritual of "anointing of the sick" have extended that ritual to help those who are suffering from serious physical illnesses—as we have seen, for a long time before it was limited to a person's dying moments. As in the Pentecostal service, in a few cases performance of this anointing ritual can have an effect on the illness itself, but this is not the principal purpose of the ritual. Rather, it is designed to combat the harm to the personhood of the sick individual. Serious sickness can usually make a person more self-centered, precisely because they have both pain and fear. The anointing ritual can and should help give the person hope, the comfort of community support, and acceptance of the creaturehood he or she shares with the rest of humanity.

Along with diseases that need curing; there are many humans who suffer from some crippling disability. Though in many cases, such as permanent blindness, there is no possibility of changing the disability, there are many things that can be done to lessen its negative effect on the life of a person. One of the more imaginative programs for doing this, and one whose effectiveness comes precisely from its use of ritual, is the Special Olympics. Many of the same sports rituals that characterize the regular Olympic games, though not as extensive, are employed to create an atmosphere of personal challenge and achievement, to give competitors a sense of importance, to make it clear that physical disabilities need not keep people from involvement in mainstream human activity.

It is not just bodily ailments that need healing. Today, probably more than at any previous period of history, millions of people throughout the world are suffering from psychological problems. Even for many who do not have psychological illness in the strict sense, there are worries and depression and fears and tensions that take away joy, peace of mind, and healthy self-confidence and seriously hinder "the pursuit of happiness." No doubt, the increased development and availability of professional psychological therapy has been a major factor in helping those with psychological problems. But there is an important place for a wide range of rituals—from family celebration to the Eucharist—that can and should work to alleviate psychological handicaps. It has been suggested that the ritual of anointing be extended to psychological as well as bodily illness, and prayers for healing already do reach out in such a way, but short of this there are many less formal human rituals, like friends sharing a meal, that can counteract loneliness, insecurity, or depression.

Of course, in many situations of psychological handicap there is no prospect of healing and a person must be helped to cope. One of these situations whose nature is much better understood today than was previously the case is that of addictions. Not too long ago, an individual's excessive use of drink or drugs was considered simply a case of immoral behavior and religious or ethical conversion was thought to be the solution. We now understand better that it is not so, that there is an unintended pattern of behavior which must be addressed by methods other than simply saying "no." Fortunately, approaches such as Alcoholics Anonymous have proved to be helpful for millions in controlling their addiction. What is important in our present discussion is the role of rituals in such programs. There is a regular ritual pattern to AA meetings, particularly a person's introduction of self by the statement, "I am so and so; I am an alcoholic." All the features of ritual are recognizable: discovery and acceptance of self-identity, formation of a community, a shared purpose, et cetera. There is demonstrated power of rituals in the control of addiction among those who persevere in the program and the lapse back into addition of many of those who discontinue participation.

Much of the need for healing has to do with relations among humans, either dysfunctional relations or lack of relations that should exist. Human society as well as individual humans is in need of healing. This is an extensive topic that we considered when we talked about reconciliation in chapter 6.

Rituals for Facing Death

Beneath all the other instances of suffering and need for healing is the "bottom line" issue of death and dying. One of the universally shared human experiences is that of suffering and death. There is a lot of truth in the old adage that there are two things certain in life, death and taxes. Humans have always feared death, tried to avoid or at least postponed it as long as possible, and tried to cope with its inevitability. We live at a time in history when medical professionals have unprecedented ability to deal with human diseases. At the same time, we have unparalleled ability to maim and kill people in war and probably have more psychological suffering than ever. We can postpone death through medical "miracles," but to a considerable extent we have lost the psychological strength to face death; in many respects, our modern culture is trying desperately to avoid confronting death.

It used to be that people took death much more for granted and handled it in the normal context of their lives (if grandpa died, it was usually at home; his body was laid out in the parlor where the wake took place; his body was brought from home to the local church and then to the cemetery) with the entire family, including the children, involved in the whole sequence. In many cases today, grandpa dies in the hospital or a nursing home, the corpse is brought to the funeral home where the wake takes place, from there to the church and then the cemetery. The entire process never touches the home. Children often are not exposed to much of this; in some cases, they are not even told that grandpa had died ("he has gone away"), with the result that they are ill-prepared for later experience of death.

In simpler times people had customary rituals for coping with, even celebrating, death. Irish wakes were jokingly described as "the corpse in the parlor and the keg in the basement." Behind this somewhat irreverent dealing with people's bereavement there was a great deal of folk wisdom. Funerals were gatherings of the whole family; at times it was the occasion for healing long-standing divisions; it was the opportunity to remember the life of the deceased with gratitude. In some cultures it was and still is customary to gather at regular intervals after the death—each month, each year—to remember the departed, to grieve together again because of him or her no longer being visibly present, and to keep alive their memory.

One of the most interesting of these after-death rituals is the annual *Día de los muertos* (Day of the Dead) that is celebrated among some Spanish-speaking people. On this day, families build little shrines at home that display mementos of the departed loved one—the person's toothbrush, binoculars, empty tequila bottle, and so on—and then they gather at the graves where they have a picnic all night long, sharing this party in spirit with those buried there. This ritual is at once a way of celebrating the lives of those who have died, a profession of belief in the after-life and of continuing relationships with the dead, and a way of people anticipating their own death as passage into the "heavenly" communion of saints.

Among official Christian rituals dealing with death, a primacy belongs to the burial service itself. All Christian groups have the practice of prayer over the burial of a member of the community. In Catholic circles this has traditionally focused on the Eucharist, on the special Requiem Mass that preceded the actual burial. This is still the case today, but there has been in recent decades a noticeable shift in the atmosphere surrounding this Eucharistic celebration. In theology about Jesus as the Christ, the past half-century has witnessed increased attention to the saving power of Jesus' resurrection instead of the previous almost exclusive focus on his death. This shift has been reflected in the tone of the Catholic funeral Mass, now called "the Mass of Resurrection." Other communities, notably the African American community of New Orleans, have long recognized burials as also occasions for celebrating the joy of resurrection.

One can grasp some of the sad solemnity that previously characterized the burial Mass when one listens to the requiems of Mozart and Cesar Franck. The requiem music was marked by the solemn gravity of the singing of the *Dies irae* (Day of Wrath), which clearly pointed to the fearsome judgment awaiting a person upon death. Today the funeral Mass is a celebration of Christian hope in risen life, a grateful prayer that the deceased loved one now enjoys resurrection in union with the risen Christ. The same is true for the burial services of Christian groups that do not have a special church service as well. More and more emphasis is placed on the joy of resurrection rather than the sorrow of passing.

This shift, incidentally, is a good illustration of one of the features of rituals that we looked at in chapter 1: rituals both reflect and shape the character of the group that is ritualizing. Whereas years ago, in services that accompanied a burial, sadness and apprehension about the afterlife reflected the outlook of those present and itself contributed to that outlook, more recent ceremonies celebrating resurrection help create and give expression to a community of grateful hope mixed with the grieving that is inescapable at death.

Rituals for Dying

Important as are rituals that help people cope with the death of loved ones, they probably are not as important as rituals that comfort and support a person who is dying. There is widespread recognition that a person should not be left alone to die, that friends and loved ones should gather to be at the bedside of a dying person, even though there may be little they can do to assist the person. Because words are so often hard to find at this time, the situation is one in which people take recourse to gestures, to rituals—they pray together; they hold the hand of the dying person; they light a candle by the bedside.

Catholics have an official ritual to accompany the actual dying of a person, the sacramental ritual of anointing joined to "viaticum" (for the journey). As we saw, for many years the anointing ritual was used exclusively for the moment of death; it was referred to as "Extreme Unction" (Last Anointing), and it was only when a person was at the point of death that a priest was called to anoint one. Even though today there is broader use of this sacramental anointing for any serious illness, it still has special application when used for a person's dying.

Along with this anointing there is the ritual of viaticum, for the last time the person is given the consecrated bread, the body of Christ in communion. Behind this ritual lies the idea that one is about to take the all-important journey into his or her lasting dwelling, that even though in faith and hope one believes that this will lead to unending joy with God, the journey is a difficult one because it is a passage into the unknown. So, in sacrament, the risen Christ, who has himself gone through this passage, joins the pilgrim to guide and support them.

A lifetime of celebrating the Eucharist is meant to prepare a dying Christian for this final ritual. At the heart of Eucharistic celebration had been the recollection of Jesus' "Passover" through death into risen life. Now, in the viaticum the ritual of Eucharist is extended to give the consecrated bread in final communion.

Popular understanding has at times looked upon the ritual of final anointing in a semi-magical way: some people have half expected it to work a miraculous cure, but this is clearly not the genuine meaning of the action. Anointing has always been a symbol of God's Spirit, and the sacramental anointing is meant to symbolize the Christian community's sharing its Spirit to empower the dying person for the supreme moment of life, to face death with calm hope in life beyond. This ritual is meant to be a public sign of the community's love and support and at the same time a profession of the community's belief in the risen Christ's triumph over death. Unfortunately, the ritual is usually done in complete privacy, with very few present. As a result, the community aspect and the human effect of community support are missing, and the ritual does not accomplish all that it is intended to.

Rituals to Alleviate Suffering

Death, however, is only part of the story. Even the happiest of lives is marked at times by suffering. It can be physical sickness, it can be psychological distress, it can be disappointment or failure, it can be the pain of rejection or betrayal by family or friends. Whatever it is, for each of us suffering makes clear a fact that we do not wish to admit: we are not in complete control. Things happen that we do not wish; sickness thwarts the plans we had and prevents achievement of our dreams. In some cases, there are years of pain for which there is no remedy.

For the vast majority of humans their abject poverty means that they never have good health. They seldom have enough to eat. They never have unpolluted water to drink. They have no decent place in which to live and raise their families. They grieve as they see the potential of their children unrealized because there is no opportunity for education. Millions of them become innocent victims of wars, killed and maimed. Millions are displaced people without a homeland, herded into refugee camps. Put quite simply, most people's lives are filled with unending suffering. One cannot avoid the question: What meaning do these lives have? What can be done to give them meaning?

When Jesus of Nazareth was faced with the suffering of so many of the people around him he had a two-pronged response. The first part of the response was quite obvious—do everything you can to alleviate the suffering. He did this by working against the suffering by feeding the hungry, healing the crippled and the lepers, consoling those who were sorrowing because of losing a loved one in death; and he encouraged others to follow his example. The second part of his response was and remains more mysterious: in his own suffering and dying he gave meaning to these by undergoing them with love for the sake of others. It is this meaning that continues to be expressed and communicated in Christian ritual.

There are many things that Christians today can do to follow Jesus' example; the particular question that concerns us in this book is whether there are ritual celebrations that can aid those who are suffering in one way or another. The answer is that celebration of Sunday prayer, of prayer over those who are ill or troubled, and of sacramental anointing have at the center of their symbolism the meaning and power of Jesus' dying and rising—that is, in various and mysterious ways, suffering can lead to fuller and deeper experience of being human, can lead to new life.

However, other rituals as well are needed in times of suffering. Almost instinctively, when friends are sick or in sorrow, we bring food or flowers— not because these friends need such things but as a sign of our sympathy, of our desire to help them bear their burden. Perhaps, though, we need more ritual ways of giving meaning to suffering. It is difficult. In most cases it is difficult to find appropriate words to express our compassion, and we end up saying and doing nothing. Rituals could be valuable to provide what words cannot. The Christian community could be more creative in expressing its concern in ritual form.

Not only do Christians need rituals to help those who are suffering, they also need rituals to strengthen and support those who are caring for the suffering. Often the care of a chronically ill or dying person is the responsibility of the family, the children or spouse of the one suffering. Care can go on for months and even years, exhausting the patience and, given the situation of health care in the United States, the financial resources of the caregiver. A striking example of this is the heartbreak of Alzheimer's disease. The Christian community could be more creative in providing rituals that acknowledge the difficulties of being a caregiver and offer the support of the community to sustain them in their struggle.[4]

Five Elements of Ritual

Hermeneutic of Experience

Most importantly, rituals of healing give meaning to the overwhelmingly debilitating experiences of human life. These rituals assert that even in its darkest hours, human life has meaning and remains sacred. As stated above, in Jesus' own suffering and dying, he gave meaning to these by undergoing them with love for the sake of others. In ways that we cannot always understand, it is love that can transform all suffering. The suffering of others can never and should never be minimized by this insight, nor should one expect or worse demand joy from those who suffer. Rather, one is called to do all one can to relieve such suffering and then hope and trust in a loving God in a way far beyond our comprehension that such pain has meaning.

Maturation

An essential part of the process of maturation is accepting one's own mortality. It is a humbling experience to realize that the world will go on without you. The experience of the death of loved one—the personal experience of loss, pain, and suffering—bring this awareness to the foreground. One appreciates more fully the beauty of the ephemeral, the sacredness of the moment. Tragedy causes us to treasure each moment given to us to love and in turn be loved. It also teaches that we are not the center of the universe. God is. We will pass, and only God and the love of God remain.

Presence

Suffering can make God more present in the two ways discussed above. First, God is present in the community that struggles to relieve suffering and to comfort those wracked by tragedy. This takes the form of physical aid, prayer, and ritual. Second, there is the more mysterious presence of the risen Christ, the one who took on suffering and death out of love and by doing so gave meaning to them, a meaning that often surpasses our understanding.

---

4. Sanchez, "A Sacred Journey."

Service

Service is so central to the Christian approach to suffering and death that there would seem no need to mention it. Christians work in many ways to relieve suffering and prevent it from happening. Included in this activity are the rituals that hope to give meaning to suffering and death, to comfort those who suffer or mourn, and to strengthen those who have succumbed to the despair of the struggle. Sometime there is no greater service than to sit quietly and hold another's hand, wordlessly waiting and hoping in love for the pain to pass.

Friendship

The fourteenth-century mystic Julian of Norwich wrote, "For always, the higher, the stronger, the sweeter that love is, the more sorrow it is to the lover to see the body which he loved in pain."[5] True friends suffer when they see their friends in pain and wish nothing so much as to take that pain away, even to take on the pain themselves. Christians should respond in the same way to the suffering around them. We should wish to take away the pain of the world when we can, to comfort those we can, and to hope that God will touch those we cannot. The rituals we have discussed celebrate that wish, empower Christians to make that wish come true and assure us that, despite all appearances, all suffering has meaning in the risen Christ.

---

5. *Julian of Norwich, Showings,* 210.

Conclusion

Christian Life as Ritual

As discussed in chapter two, rituals are necessarily linked to relationships of power within a society. It should not come as a surprise, therefore, that rituals themselves can be and have been ranked according to those who have the power to perform them. After all, those who perform the rituals have a vested interest in emphasizing the importance of what they do. So those rituals performed by "professionals"—priests, ministers, deacons, and so on—are classified as the "official" or even the only rituals of Christianity. Most books that describe Christian "sacraments" assume that only these official rituals are worth discussing.

There are many other important Christian rituals and symbols, however, that can be much more important to individual Christians than the "official" rituals we has so far discussed. In an older terminology, these rituals and symbols would have been called "sacramentals" in distinction from the official rituals or sacraments. In fact, the line between "official" and "unofficial" or "popular" rituals is historically rather porous. Coronation of kings and queens was once considered an "official" ritual, while for centuries marriage was not. The slow movement of these changes is often measured in millennia since societies are very conservative about ritual actions or symbols. Yet the change does occur as power shifts occur within a society.

In this chapter we discuss rituals that are not "official" but are very important and often more central for the faith life of certain communities and of particular individuals than the official rites. They are ordinarily not performed or controlled by professionals—that is, ministers, priests, or other paid practitioners. Rather, the celebrants of these rituals are ordinary Christians in their everyday lives. Yet they are so powerful within their communities that they can symbolize and even help define those communities.

Quince Años

In several Latin American societies, and particularly in Mexican and Mexican American culture, the coming of age of a young women is cause for great celebration. The ceremony is known as *quince años* (fifteenth birthday) or more commonly, *quinceañera*, referring both to the ceremony and the young girl celebrating the ritual. The central feature of the *quinceañera* is a large party and dance, similar to a coming-out party or debutante ball. The affair is quite expensive, and preparations are elaborate. There are at present well over 10,000 Web sites dedicated to providing a *quinceañera* and her family with religious items, clothing, how-to-books, fiesta products, receptions, and even cruises.[1]

The *quinceañera* is more than just a coming-out party though; it is a religious ceremony as well. Before the fiesta begins, there is a church ceremony that, as least for the Roman Catholics who make up the majority of the *quinceañeras* and their families, takes place in the midst of the Eucharistic liturgy. There is even an official liturgy for the ceremony, approved by Archbishop Patricio Flores of the Roman Catholic diocese of San Antonio, Texas.[2] This places the *quinceañera* in an awkward situation: it is both a popular ceremony and an official rite. The ritual also crosses denominational boundaries and is practiced by Baptists, Lutherans, and Anglicans, as well as Roman Catholics. Perhaps in another hundred years, it will become a "sacrament" or official ceremony of Christianity, somewhat like confirmation, another coming of age ritual.

The religious part of the ritual consists of the usual liturgy of the Mass with special readings suggested for the ceremony: "The service begins with a procession of the Court of Honor, which may consist of fifteen couples: the

---

1. Theresa Torres, "*La Quinceañera*: Traditioning and the Social Construction of the Mexican American Female," in Orlando O. Espín and Gary Macy, eds., *The Future of Our Past: Explorations in the Theology of Tradition* (Maryknoll, NY: Orbis Books, 2006). Dr. Torres's article was very helpful in describing the *quinceañera*.

2. The official text is contained in *Quinceañera: Celebración de la vida, guía para los que presiden el rito religioso / Quinceañera: Celebration of Life: Guidebook for the Presider of the Religious Rite* (San Antonio, TX: Mexican American Cultural Center, 1999). The guidebook includes an excellent introduction to this ritual by Fr. Raúl Gómez.

damas (young women) and the *chambelanes* (young men), followed by *la quin-ceañera* with her escort (a *chambelán* or her father) and the priest."[3] After the homily, the *quinceañeras* renew their baptismal vows in front of the congrega-tion and profess their faith. A song of commitment follows, as do special in-tercessions for the young women. As the altar is prepared, special symbols are carried up to the altar along with the bread and wine. These can include gifts that have been given to the *quinceañera* by her *padrinos* (sponsors) such as a religious medal (usually of Mary, often of Our Lady of Guadalupe), a rosary, and a Bible or missal. Other gifts are sometimes blessed: a doll, crown, high heels, pillow, and roses. Other symbols may also be used that indicate a con-tinued dedication to the faith, including baptismal certificates, baptismal robes, baptismal shoes, and baptismal candles. Finally at the end of the service, the *quinceañeras* consecrate themselves to God and to Our Lady of Guadalupe. The young women are blessed by their parents, and a concluding rite ends in song. From here, the festivities move to the formal dance and reception.

The *quinceañera* stands in a middle ground between official and unofficial, popular status. It has an official rite, yet much of the ceremony is determined and controlled by the family and friends of the *quinceañera*. It is perhaps the best contemporary example of an important ritual that straddles the artificial division between official and unofficial rites.

Images: Icons, Pictures, and Statues

Christians have had their disagreements about the use of religious art. Begin-ning in the seventh century, some Christians began to doubt the value of rep-resentations of sacred scenes, objects, and persons. In the eighth and ninth centuries, certain of the Byzantine emperors even struggled to eliminate the use of religious pictures and statues in Eastern Christianity. The effort was ultimately unsuccessful, and despite a renewal of iconoclasm (destruction of images) among some sixteenth-century Reformers, on the whole, Christians have found religious images and statues extremely important in their daily lives.

The use of religious art can take many forms in Christianity. In the Eastern Orthodox churches, icons (stylized religious paintings) have an extremely im-portant role. The saints, Mary, and even Jesus are thought to operate through the icons that contain their stylized images. Through the mediation of the

3. Torres, *"La Quinceañera."*

icons, they preside at important events in life, protect the community in which the icons reside, and cure and comfort those who venerate them through the images. Out of respect, the icons are kissed and incensed, a devout person may prostrate herself or himself before them. The creation of an icon is itself a sacred act, requiring not only great skill but also prayer and devotion. Again, the roles that icons have in the devotional and ritual life of Orthodoxy equals or surpasses the importance of some "official" rituals.

A similar part is played by some central images in Western Christianity. For Poles, the image of Our Lady of Czestochowa represents the care Mary has for the Polish people. The same can be said for the image of Our Lady of Guadalupe for Mexicans and for the stature of Our Lady of Charity for Cubans. These images are the focus not only of religious devotion but also of national identity. There are many other examples of such images. They find their way into homes, medals, cars, and even clothes or tattoos. The feast days to such images are extremely important. In each case, the divine is understood to operate through such images, particularly aiding those nations who honor and are honored by the images. Usually the origin of the images is miraculous, a sign of God's favor to a particular group of people. To attack the image or to question the miraculous nature of its origins would be not just to dishonor the devotion of the people but to question the honor and integrity of their culture.

Receptive of less fervor, but also important, are popular religious pictures. Photos of the "praying hands" or of prints of Jesus with long, flowing blond hair and beard, or reproductions of DaVinci's Last Supper appear in thousands of homes across the United States and around the world. The ubiquitous presence of these images demonstrates the devotion of those who display them in their homes. These images may not themselves be the focus of devotion, but they do symbolize the religious beliefs of their owners in an important way.

The Bible

The sacred book of Christianity is accorded a veneration quite apart from the words contained therein. The cover and pages of the book have been and often continue to be elaborately decorated. The Bible is carried in processions into liturgy and is carefully guarded from neglect or accident. Many families pass the same Bible down from generation to generation; in fact, the family Bible often contains a record of those generations in its flyleaves. Politicians swear their inaugural oaths on the Bible, and the witnesses in court swear to tell "the truth, the whole truth, and nothing but the truth" with their hand placed on the Bible. The physical object of the Bible is a vital focus for devotion for many Christians in and of itself.

Certain translations of the Bible can also become iconic. The language of the King James version of the Bible was once the everyday language of the English people, but in all other areas of life, such language has long been abandoned. Not for some Christian groups, however: they understand this translation to be divinely inspired and consider any other translation of the Bible an abandonment of the true faith. Some probably believe that Jesus, the apostles, and even God actually used "thee" and "thou" when they spoke. To suggest that the original Hebrew and Greek don't necessarily carry such formality is tantamount to heresy. The Latin Vulgate translation of the Bible for centuries carried the same symbolic value for Roman Catholics. In these cases, a translation becomes somehow divinely inspired and worthy of veneration in itself.

In these cases, both the Bible as an object and particular translations of the Bible are understood to mediate the divine presence. They have value and power in and of themselves. For many Christians, then, the Bible has a far more important symbolic role than any particular church ritual or even, perhaps, than the message contained in that book.

Sacred Places

The obvious sacred places for Christians are churches. Christians gather in churches to celebrate all the ceremonies discussed above. They wander into churches to offer a silent prayer or ask for help from God. Churches are clearly holier than other places. For centuries, most countries have even recognized the right of sanctuary within a church. Anyone who flees to a church may not be dragged from it, even if they are clearly guilty of crimes. People who have rarely, if ever, attended any official Christian liturgies and who certainly do not consider themselves part of any Christian community feel that it is very important that they marry in a church. They may even later feel the need to baptize their children in a church and will quite likely be buried from a church. For Christians, then, even nominal ones, churches have a special divine presence.

Particular churches have more symbolic power than others. Churches associated with great events in Christian history, especially the events of Jesus' life, attract pilgrims from all over the world. Churches where great saints are buried, or where treasured images are kept, also attract thousands of the faithful who come to be in a sacred space, a place where God is more available.

Especially popular are churches or sites where miracles or cures have occurred. Pilgrims gather to pray and hope that they too might partake of the divine mercy of healing.

Pilgrimages—that is, journeys undertaken to sacred sites for a religious reason—have long played an important part in Christianity. The most famous pilgrimage sites are Jerusalem, Bethlehem, and Nazareth, the places of Jesus' birth and ministry. Of nearly equal importance for some Western Christians is Rome, the place of the death of St. Peter and St. Paul. For Roman Catholics, Rome is also the place where the pope, the head of the church, resides. Other important pilgrimage sites include the burial place of St. James the Apostle in Compostela, Spain, and the many places where Mary the mother of Jesus is believed to have appeared: Lourdes, Fatima, Medjugorje, and Guadalupe. Many people save their whole lives for a trip to these centers of devotion or even make the trip on foot to show their devotion.

Not all sacred spaces are in churches, however. Many Christians have home shrines and altars. This may be quite simple: a statue of a saint and a candle, for example. Such shrines can also be very elaborate, however, with pictures of a deceased family member along with religious images and symbols. There might be a place in the house where the Bible is kept on a special stand, and it is here that the family gathers for scripture reading each night. In all these cases, the risen Christ is felt as present within the home, blessing and caring for all those within.

Altars can also be created outside the home. Roadside shrines mark the spot where a loved one died in an accident. Fresh flowers, a cross, or a stature might ordain such spots. Recently, a related practice has spontaneously appeared at places of great tragedy, as in the case of the Oklahoma bombing or the shootings at Columbine. Most dramatically, New York City spent months planning a suitable memorial to replace the twin towers of the World Trade Center. People bring poems, presents, pictures, letters, candles, and flowers to the site of the tragedy. Although the action is predominately secular in nature, there is a religious dimension to the practice that makes it worth mentioning. Perhaps such memorials will become ordinary rituals in American society. If so, it would be very surprising if they did not contain an explicitly religious dimension.

Sacred Clothes

Christians most obviously don sacred clothes when they gather for Sunday prayer. The people in the pew often put on dress clothes of some sort. The minister, however, really shines. The garments he or she wears most often are modified clothes from the fourth century. Long gowns, stoles, and tunics adorn the celebrant. The colors may range from a somber black to glorious red, gold, and azure, but the celebrant is clearly marked out by sacred clothes. The choir can also don equally spectacular garb. Special clothes demarcate the special standing of those who lead the celebration.

Some ministers also wear distinctive garb outside the liturgical celebration. Often these clothes come from another historical period. The most popular clothes for clerics are a form of either sixteenth- or nineteenth-century dress, usually a somber and simple black cassock or suit. Clerics are not the only Christians who wear distinctive dress in public. Some Christian groups deliberately wear very plain clothes, again based on models from earlier centuries, the most obvious example being the Amish. Religious communities can have a distinctive dress that reminds them of their founders. Franciscans, for example, wear simple woolen robes with a rope for a belt and sandals because this was the poorest form of clothing in the thirteenth century and much favored by St. Francis and his early followers. Other religious orders founded in the sixteenth or nineteenth centuries favor dress popular in those eras. This dress is traditionally called a "habit," and the decision to stop wearing the habit and adopt simple but current clothing can be the cause of tremendous controversy.

Simpler and less obvious religious ornamentation includes medals or crosses worn on a chain around the neck. One form of such attire, the scapular, consists of two small pieces of cloth worn on the back and front and joined by string. Although not as popular as they were in the past, scapulars are sometimes still worn to identify oneself as an admirer or adherent of a particular religious order, the scapular being a kind of "mini-habit." Of course, crosses are also worn as earrings, pins, or various kinds of body ornament and do not necessarily indicate any kind of religious devotion or affiliation at all. Yet, many Christians do wear jewelry that is meant to proclaim their devotion. Tee shirts can do so even more blatantly, as can backpacks or caps. Christians can literally wear their beliefs on their sleeves.

Christians for centuries have demonstrated their devotion in dress, and the twenty-first century gives every indication that proclivity is alive and well. The way this is done has changed and will continue to do so, but one can well imagine Christian spacesuits lurking somewhere in our future.

Private Prayer

It goes almost without saying that Christians do a great deal of praying outside any official ritual. The most common times for prayer (apart from crisis) are first thing in the morning, last thing at night, and whenever one stops to eat. It is not uncommon to see devout Christians in a restaurant stop and pray before a meal, perhaps making the sign of the cross (touching the forehead, the chest, and alternately each of the shoulders).

A more elaborate form of daily prayer is the "divine office." In this very old style of prayer, dating back at least to the fourth century, a devout Christian prays up to eight times a day. The pattern can vary, but one form would contain the following prayers: Matins at 2:30 A.M.; Lauds at 6:00 A.M.; Prime at 6:45 A.M.; Terce at 8:00 A.M.; Sext at 12:00 noon; None at 1:30 P.M.; Vespers at 4:15 P.M.; and finally, Compline at 6:15 P.M. This complete set of the divine office was reserved to professional religious whose life revolved around these prayers. Many ordinary Christians, however, have adopted a modified form of daily prayer that follows, more or less, the more elaborate office mentioned above. Vespers, for instance, is often celebrated by the entire community in the Episcopalian tradition.

Less elaborate forms of prayer are often practiced at home by Christians as well. Some families read the Bible together each evening or gather for prayer and scripture. Prayer may precede a car trip. Parents may bless their children when they leave the house. Some people have the entire house blessed when they first move in. Pets, too, can receive a special blessing. All in all, Christians pray a lot.

Not surprisingly, Christians wish their entire lives to be dedicated to the life of the risen Christ. In such a world, there is no separation between the sacred and the secular. Everything is God's world; everything is graced by the love of God. All in all, Christians have thousands of ways of demonstrating their beliefs and practicing those beliefs that fall outside the official rituals that make up community celebrations. This book has touched on only some of those rituals. It is up to the reader to discover others, to invent others if he or she is Christian. It is up to everyone to celebrate life, and that means to ritualize.

Act, dress, vest; talk, laugh, cry, growl, roar, complain, explain, whisper, sing out loud; push, pull, carry, lug, dig, sand, weld, file, press, read, write, call, type, lecture, sell, buy; shake hands, hug, kiss, embrace, gently touch your child's cheek; glance, stare, peer, examine, read; eat, drink, sup, dine, sip, slurp, gulp; dance, walk, skip, trip, fall, sit, lounge, and sleep like the person you truly wish you were, and chances are you will become that person. Hang around with people who are similar to what you wish you were, and chances are you will become those people. For all our sake, for the sake of the world, for your own sake, choose to be, and be with, people who are loving. Be joyful when you can, be gracious when you can't, and when you can't be either, at least try to act like you can. You might be amazed at what you have become.

Or, to put it in the language of Christianity, let the risen Christ shine through you. For those so blessed, every breath is a sacrament.

Suggestions for Further Reading

Bausch, William. *A New Look at the Sacraments*. Rev. ed. Mystic, CT: Twenty-Third Publications, 1983.

Bell, Catherine. *Ritual Theory: Ritual Practice*. New York: Oxford University Press, 1992.

Bernier, Paul. *Ministry in the Church: A Historical and Pastoral Approach*. Mystic, CT: Twenty-Third Publications, 1992.

Cooke, Bernard. *The Future of the Eucharist: How a New Self-Awareness among Catholics Is Changing the Way They Believe and Worship*. New York: Paulist Press, 1997.

Cooke, Bernard. *Reconciled Sinners: Healing Human Brokenness*. Mystic, CT: Twenty-Third Publications, 1986.

Cooke, Bernard. *Sacraments and Sacramentality*. Rev. ed. Mystic, CT: Twenty-Third Publications, 1994.

Dallen, James. *The Reconciling Community: The Rite of Penance*. Collegeville, MN: Liturgical Press, 1986.

Davis, Kenneth G., ed. *Misa, Mesa y Musa: Liturgy in the U. S. Hispanic Church*, 2nd ed. Schiller Park, IL: World Library Publications, 1997.

Elizondo, Virgil, and Sean Freyne, eds. *Pilgrimage*. Maryknoll, NY: Orbis Books, 1996.

Empereur, James. *Prophetic Anointing: God's Call to the Sick, the Elderly, and the Dying*. Wilmington, DE: Michael Glazier, 1982.

Fink, Peter. *Praying the Sacraments*. Washington, DC: Pastoral Press, 1991.

Grimes, Ronald. *Beginnings in Ritual Studies*. Washington, D.C.: University Press of America, 1982.

Gruber, Howard E., and J. Jacques Vonèche, eds. *The Essential Piaget*. New York: Basic Books, 1977.

Gula, Richard. *To Walk Together Again: The Sacrament of Reconciliation.* New York: Paulist Press, 1984.

Gusmer, Charles. *And You Visited Me: Sacramental Ministry to the Sick and Dying.* Rev. ed. New York: Pueblo, 1989.

Guzie, Tad. *The Book of Sacramental Basics.* New York: Paulist Press, 1981.

Hellwig, Monica. *Sign of Reconciliation and Conversion: The Sacrament of Penance for Our Times.* Wilmington, DL: Michael Glazier, 1982.

House, H. Wayne, ed. *Divorce and Remarriage: Four Christian Views.* Downers Grove, IL: InterVarsity, 1990.

Jones, Cheslyn, Geoffrey Wainwright, Edward Yarnold, and Paul Bradshaw. *The Study of Liturgy.* Rev. ed. New York: Oxford University Press, 1992.

Kavanagh, Aidan. *The Shape of Baptism: The Rite of Christian Initiation.* New York: Pueblo, 1978.

Kelsey, Morton. *Healing and Christianity.* Minneapolis, MN: Augburg, 1995.

Kennedy, Robert, ed. *Reconciliation: The Continuing Agenda.* Collegeville, MN: Liturgical Press, 1987.

Kilmartin, Edward. *The Eucharist in the West: History and Theology.* Collegeville, MN: Liturgical Press, 1998.

Langer, Susanne. *Philosophy in a New Key: A Study in the Symbolism of Reason, Rite, and Art.* Cambridge, MA: Harvard University Press, 1957.

Lawler, Michael. *Marriage and the Catholic Church: Disputed Questions.* Collegeville, MN: Liturgical Press, 2002.

Lawler, Michael. *Symbol and Sacrament: A Contemporary Sacramental Theology.* Omaha, NE: Creighton University Press, 1995.

Lawler, Michael. *A Theology of Ministry.* Kansas City, MO: Sheed and Ward, 1990.

Lawler, Michael, and Thomas Shanahan. *Church: A Spirited Communion.* Collegeville, MN: Liturgical Press, 1995.

Lawler, Michael, and William Roberts, eds. *Christian Marriage and Family: Contemporary Theological and Pastoral Problems.* Collegeville, MN: Liturgical Press, 1996.

Lee, Bernard. *Alternative Futures for Worship,* vol. 5: *Christian Marriage.* Collegeville, MN: Liturgical Press, 1987.

Macy, Gary. *The Banquet's Wisdom: A Short History of the Lord's Supper.* 2nd ed. Akron, OH: OSL Publications, 2005.

Maddocks, Morris. *The Christian Healing Ministry.* London: SPCK, 1981.

Mazza, Enrico. *The Celebration of the Eucharist: The Origins of the Rite and the Development of the Interpretation.* Collegeville, MN: Liturgical Press, 1999.

Mitchell, Nathan. *Liturgy and the Social Sciences.* Collegeville, MN: Liturgical Press, 1999.

Noll, Ray. *Sacraments: A New Understanding for a New Generation.* Mystic, CT: Twenty-Third Publications, 1999.

O'Meara, Thomas. *Theology of Ministry.* Rev. ed. New York: Paulist Press, 1999.

Osborne, Kenan. *Christian Sacraments of Initiation: Baptism, Confirmation, Eucharist.* New York: Paulist Press, 1987.

Osborne, Kenan. *Ministry: Lay Ministry in the Roman Catholic Church: Its History and Theology.* New York: Paulist Press, 1993.

Osborne, Kenan. *Reconciliation and Justification: The Sacrament and Its Theology*. New York: Paulist Press, 1990.

Perrin, David. *The Sacrament of Reconciliation: An Existential Approach*. Lewiston, NY: Edwin Mellen Press, 1998.

Power, David N. *The Eucharistic Mystery: Revitalizing the Tradition*. New York: Crossroad, 1992.

Powers, Joseph. *Spirit and Sacrament: The Humanizing Experience*. New York: Seabury, 1973.

Rademacher, William . *Lay Ministry: A Theological, Spiritual and Pastoral Handbook*. New York: Crossroad, 2002.

Rahner, K. *The Church and the Sacraments*. New York: Herder and Herder, 1963.

Ross, Susan. *Extravagant Affections: A Feminist Sacramental Theology*. New York: Continuum, 1998.

Rutherford, Richard, and Tony Barr. *The Death of a Christian: The Order of Christian Funerals*. Rev. ed. Collegeville, MN: Liturgical Press, 1990.

Schillebeeckx, E. *Christ: The Sacrament of the Encounter with God*. New York: Sheed and Ward, 1963.

Schillebeeckx, Edward. *The Eucharist*. New York: Sheed and Ward, 1968.

Seaholtz, R. Kevin, ed. *Living Bread, Saving Cup: Readings on the Eucharist*. Collegeville, MN: Liturgical Press, 1982.

Susin, Luiz Carlos, and María Pilar Aquino. *Reconciliation in a World of Conflicts*. London: SCM Press, 2003.

Thomas, David. *Christian Marriage: A Journey Together*. Collegeville, MN: Liturgical Press, 1988.

Thurian, Max, and Geoffrey Wainwright, eds. *Baptism and Eucharist: Ecumenical Convergence in Celebration*. Grand Rapids, MI: Eerdmans, 1983.

Wainwright, Geoffrey. *Eucharist and Eschatology*. New York: Oxford University Press, 1981.

White, James. *Protestant Worship: Traditions in Transition*. Louisville, KY: Westminister/ John Knox, 1989.

Wright, Nancy, and Donald Kill. *Ecological Healing: A Christian Vision*. Maryknoll, NY: Orbis, 1993.

Zibawi, Mahmoud. *The Icon: Its Meaning and History*. Collegeville, MN: Liturgical Press, 1993.

Index

Abba, 40, 41
abbess, 136
abbesses, 115
abbot, 115, 136
Acacius of Amida, 150
acolyte, 127, 132
adultery, 66, 68, 111
Alexandria, 130, 133, 135
alienation, 109–111, 117
altar, 99, 163
    altar call, 98, 112
    home altar 23, 166
ambiguity, 23–24, 46, 142
Ammianus Marcellinus, 130 n. 5
anamnesis, 44, 92
Anglican, 97, 162. *See also* Episcopalian
annulment, 67–68
anointing, 47, 59, 78
    in baptism, 73–74, 78, 82–84
    in civil ceremonies, 132, 135
    in confirmation, 78
    of the sick, 150–152, 155–157
Antioch, 130, 133, 135
apostasy, 111
apostle, 36, 71, 123–124. See also *apostolos*
apostolicity, 123–124
apostolos, 36, 123–124, 126. *See also* apostle
Armenian Church, 131, 133
ascetics, 129, 131, 136, 138, 143
askesis, 128
Assyrian Church, 133
Augustine of Hippo, 73, 97, 129

baptism, 37–38, 46, 49, 69–71, 73–86, 104,
    111–112, 140

Baptist, 81, 83, 97, 102, 162
Basil of Caesaria, 149–150
Bethlehem, 166
Bible, 35–36, 60, 94–96, 100–102, 109,
    147, 163–166, 168
bishop, 28, 36, 73, 75, 78, 84, 92, 100, 112,
    125–127, 129–135, 137–138, 140–142.
    See also *episcopos*
body of Christ, 23, 44–45, 53, 96–97, 105,
    107, 155
bread, 23, 37–38, 43, 46, 71–72, 87–102,
    105, 107, 145, 155–156, 163
burial, 154–155, 166

Cambridge, 100
Cana, 39–40
catechumenate, 81–82
Cathars, 99
celibacy, 100, 136–137
Chadwick, Henry, 127, 149
chambelán, 163
Charlemagne, 120, 135
Christopher, 48
Church of Christ, Scientist, 150
clergy, 22, 24, 133, 136–141, 151
collection at liturgy, 88, 98
communion, reception of, 67, 71, 80, 84,
    89, 97–98, 107, 155–156. *See also*
    Eucharist
    first, 80, 84
    of churches, 125, 133–135, 140
    of saints, 154
Compostela, 166
confession of sin, 104, 112–116
confirmation, 47, 78–80, 84, 162

congregationalists, 142
Constantine, 75, 129
Constantinople, 130, 133, 135
Coptic church, 133
Council of Nicea, 67, 130
Council of Trent, 59
Cranmer, Thomas, 100, 100 n. 4, 101
cross, 162, 167
   sign of, 73, 168
Crusades, 142
Czestochowa, Our Lady of, 164

deacon, 36, 73–74, 88, 126–127, 130, 132, 134,
   136, 139, 144, 161. See also *diakonos*
deaconess, 74, 132
death, 7–8, 11–12, 23, 26, 32–33, 49, 52, 57, 61,
   65, 70–71, 75, 91, 94, 100 n. 4, 129, 130 n.
   5, 144, 147, 157–159, 166
   of Jesus, 35, 41–42, 44, 48–49, 61, 70–71, 83,
      87, 90, 92–93, 104
   rituals for, 31, 47, 147–148, 151, 153–156
Día de los muertos, 154
diakonos, 36, 126. See also deacon
disciple, 36, 40–42, 46–47, 70, 74, 86, 90, 109–
   110, 146, 148. See also *discipolos*
Disciples of Christ, 81
discipolos, 36, 124
dissolution of marriage, 66–68
divine office, 168

Easter, 73, 80, 82, 114
Easter Vigil, 73, 82
Eastern Christians, 94
Eastern Orthodox, 67, 84, 89, 97, 101–102, 126,
   133, 141, 163
Eddy, Mary Baker, 150
Egypt, 91, 94, 128, 147
elder, 36, 125, 139, 150. See also presbyter;
   presbyteros
emperor, 22, 75, 130, 132, 135, 137, 163
empress, 22
episcopate, 126–128, 142
Episcopalian, 101–102, 134, 145, 168. See also
   Anglican
episcopos, 36, 73, 125. See also bishop
Ethiopian Church, 131, 133
Eucharist, 30, 37–38, 43–44, 46–47, 49, 65, 71,
   74, 80, 87–107, 112, 116, 152, 154, 156,
   162. See also communion, reception of
evil, 40–43, 47–49, 76–77, 83, 93, 100, 116–118,
   143, 147–148, 151
ex voto, 151
excommunication, 97, 107, 135
Exodus, 93
exomologesis, 111–112
exorcism in baptism, 73
exorcist, 127, 132, 152
extreme unction, 151, 155

Fabiola of Rome, 149–150
fasting, 72–73, 100, 112, 128
Fatima, 166
Francis of Assisi, 167
funeral, 11, 58, 102, 154–155

George of Alexandria, 130–131, 130 n. 5
godparents, 49, 73–75, 77, 79–80, 82, 85
grace, 49–53, 84, 125, 127, 168
graduation, 21, 24, 26–27, 58, 62
Gregory I, 134
Guadalupe, Our Lady of, 163–164, 166

habit, as religious dress, 167
Haight, John, 39
hands, laying on of, 74, 78, 122, 132, 140
handshake, 32, 56, 110–111, 113
Henry VIII, 101
hermeneutic of experience, 52–53, 64, 85, 104,
   116, 144, 158
hiereus, 128. See also priest
homily, 84, 122, 163
hospital, 149, 154
Hugh of St. Victor, 37

iconoclasm, 163
icons, 163–164
images, religious, 39, 163–165
Inquisition, 142
Islam, 64, 135
Israel, 39, 46, 60, 74, 111, 123, 147

James, Letter of, 150–151
Jerusalem, 111, 130, 133, 135, 147, 166
John the Apostle, 126
   Gospel of, 39–40, 43, 46, 48, 51, 61, 70, 75, 145–
      146
   Letter of, 51, 106
John the Baptist, 70
Judaism, 40, 49, 60, 63, 70, 123, 142
Judas, 123
Julian of Norwich, 50, 159
Justin Martytr, 72–73, 88–89, 92, 95, 99

king, 22, 136, 161
King James Bible, 35–36, 165

laity, 22, 24, 136–141
Langer, Susan, 6, 6 n. 1, 7
lector, 133, 136
Leo I, 133–134
limbo, 76
liturgy, 7, 80, 82, 95, 98, 101–103, 112, 115–116,
   121, 124, 129, 151, 162, 164
Lord's Supper. See communion, reception of;
   Eucharist
Lourdes, 166
Luke, Gospel of, 87–88, 123–124

Luther, Martin, 100, 100 n. 4, 101, 115, 138–140, 143
Lutheran, 97, 100–102, 115, 126, 139, 162

magic, 47, 49, 77, 148
Mar Thomas Syrian Church, 133
Marcionites, 124–125, 125 n. 1
Mark, Gospel of, 66–67, 87, 123
marriage, 14, 28–30, 38–39, 44, 52, 58–61, 63–68, 79, 129, 132, 136–138, 143–144, 161
Mary, the mother of Jesus, 163–164, 166
Mary Magdalene, 120
Mass, 23, 89, 100, 154–155, 162
Matthew, Gospel of, 41–42, 53, 66, 68, 70, 87, 111, 116, 123
medals, religious, 164, 167
Medjugorje, 166
Messiah, 36, 41, 91, 93
Messianic banquet, 93
Methodist, 97
missionaries, 100, 123–124, 126
monasticism, 128
monk, 114–115, 129, 132, 136
Montanists, 125, 125 n. 1
mysterion, 37, 39

Nazareth, 166
Norman, Ruth and Ernest, 120–122
normative periods in history, 133–134, 138, 142
novena, 151
nun, 115, 136, 139

orders, religious, 150, 167
ordinatio, ordinationes, 28, 132, 136, 146. See also ordination
ordination, 22, 28, 47, 63, 100 n. 4, 112, 116, 121–122, 130–133, 136, 138–142, 144, 166
ordo, ordines, 28, 132, 135–136. See also ordination
Our Lady of Charity, 164

padrinos, 163
papacy, 100, 136–138. See also pope
Passover, 87, 90–91, 156
pastor, 63, 78, 139
patriarch, 101, 130–131, 133–135
Paul, the apostle, 124, 166
    the letters of, 40–41, 60, 67, 70, 85, 87–88, 97, 110, 123, 130
Pauline privilege, 67
penance, 67, 98, 104, 112, 114–115
Pentecostal, 7, 151–152
Persian Empire, 131, 134, 150
Peter, the apostle, 71, 148, 166
Peter the Lombard, 38, 59
Petrine privilege, 67
Piaget, Jean, 16
pilgrimage, 114, 148, 156, 165–166

Polycarp of Smyrna, 126
pope, 67, 101, 127, 130, 135, 137–138, 140–142, 166. See also papacy
porneia, 66
power and ritual, 20–23, 28–30, 103, 137, 142–146, 161
Presbyterian, 125, 142
presbyteros, 36, 73, 125–127. See also elder; presbyter
presbyter, 73, 125–127, 129–130, 132–133. See also elder; presbyteros
presence of Christ in Christian ritual, 20, 22–24, 37–38, 44–45, 88–89, 93–94, 96–103, 105, 107, 145, 158
priest, 7, 23, 36, 60, 63, 73, 84, 100, 103, 112, 115, 122, 125, 128, 134–136, 138, 140, 155, 161–163. See also sacerdos
procession, 11, 98, 151, 162, 164
procreation and marriage, 28, 30
profession of faith, 83

queen, 22, 136, 161
quince años, quinceañera, 162–163

readers, order of, 127, 132
Reformation of the sixteenth century, 37–38, 81, 87, 89, 94–96, 100–101, 112, 125, 137–141, 151, 163
Reformed Christianity, 84, 94, 101, 112, 139–141. See also Reformation of the sixteenth century
remarriage, 68
resurrection, 42–45, 48–49, 61–62, 70, 83, 90, 93, 104–105, 114, 154–155
Roman Catholic, 23, 38, 89, 101–103, 112, 120, 126, 129, 131, 137–138, 151, 154–155, 162, 165–166
    baptism, 81–84
    dissolution of marriage. See annulment
    ministry, 140–142
    reconciliation, 155–156
Rome, 13, 72, 88, 101, 127, 130, 134–135, 137–138, 149–150, 166
Ross, Susan, 23–24

sacerdos, 128. See also priest
sacrament, 24, 36–39, 43–46, 49–52, 59–63, 66–67, 84, 110–111, 136, 141, 155–157, 161–162, 169. See also sacramentum
sacramentum, 14, 36–39. See also sacrament
sacrifice, 10–11, 41, 44, 66, 90–92, 111, 128
saint, 31, 40, 48, 110, 151, 154, 163, 165–167
salvation, 31, 38, 41–43, 49–50, 52–53, 59–60, 62, 72, 76–77, 81, 89, 93, 95, 105, 141–142, 147. See also savior
Sanchez, Cathleen, 92 n. 2, 158 n. 4
sanctuary, 165
Satan, 49, 82

savior, 36, 42–43, 46. *See also* salvation
scapular, 167
science, 9, 41, 48
Second Vatican Council, 7, 81, 115
Seder, 30, 90
shrines, 23, 154, 166
sin, 42–43, 48–49, 52, 67–68, 72, 75–76, 81–83, 89, 94, 97–98, 104, 109–118, 147–148, 151
slavery, 91, 143
Socrates, 120, 150
Spirit of God, 40–41, 43, 47–49, 70–75, 77–79, 83–86, 97–98, 110–111, 125, 148, 156
sports, 5–6, 56, 152
statue, religious, 151, 163, 166
subdeacon, 127, 136
Sunday, 7, 58, 71, 73, 80, 88–89, 96–98, 102, 112, 115, 140, 145, 151, 157, 166
synagogue, 94, 125
Syrian church, 36, 74, 124, 128, 133

temple, 71, 90–92, 111, 147–148
Thanksgiving, 21, 30, 31
Thomas Aquinas, 37–38

Torres, Theresa, 162–163
transubstantiation, 100–101
Twelve, the, 123–124, 148

Unarius Academy of Science, 121

Vespers, 168
vestments, 129, 132
viaticum, 155–156
virgins, order of, 129, 132

wake, for the dead, 153–154
wedding, 29–30, 47, 59–60, 62–66, 77, 120
Western Christianity, 14, 76, 80, 94, 100–101, 114, 129, 134–136, 140–141, 164, 166
widow, 88, 127, 129, 132, 149
wine, 23, 37–39, 43, 46, 72–73, 88–90, 92–101, 105, 107, 128, 145, 163
Word of God, 40, 43, 46, 89, 94–96

Zoroasterian, 131
Zwingli, Ulrich, 100–101